STARING AT CEILINGS

JONATHAN JAMES KAY

with

BRENDA ANN KAY

STARING AT CEILINGS

Matador
9 De Montfort Mews
Leicester LE1 7FW, UK
Tel: (+44) 116 255 9311 / 9312
Email: books@troubador.co.uk
Web: www.troubador.co.uk/matador

ISBN 1 904744 89 3

Cover illustration: © Photos.com

Typeset in 11pt Stempel Garamond by Troubador Publishing Ltd, Leicester, UK
Printed by The Cromwell Press, Trowbridge, Wilts, UK

Matador is an imprint of Troubador Publishing

CONTENTS

ACKNOWLEDGEMENTS

Thanks go to Barry Quinn and Patrick Ness for their invaluable contributions to this book... and of course, to all of you who joined us on our difficult journey.

A journey made possible through research...

Proceeds from the sale of this book will be donated to Leukaemia Research (registered charity 216032).

INTRODUCTION

Barry Quinn MSc BD Bacc Phil RN*

In 1998, there were fifty-five million people living in the United Kingdom and in that same year 306,365 people were diagnosed with cancer. Behind each of these figures lies a person with a story to tell, and each story is worth listening to.

I have heard many people with cancer tell their story at different times and different places, sometimes during the night when the ward is quiet or when I've been carrying out a clinical task such as administering chemotherapy or dressing a wound. All these stories have something in common: others may come and go, but it is only the storyteller who has been there from the beginning.

Oscar Wilde once said that where there is sorrow there you will find holy ground and we will know nothing of life until we face that fact. That is not to say that every account of cancer bears sorrow. The good news is that as the number of people being diagnosed with cancer rises, the survival rates continue to improve.

But while cancer is a medical diagnosis, sometimes health care workers such as myself can become so involved in the medical diagnosis that we fail to listen to the stories of those we care for.

Of the 306,365 people diagnosed with cancer in 1998, 2583 were diagnosed with Lymphoid Leukaemia a very rare cancer of the blood. Of those number diagnosed, thirty-seven were young men in their twenties. One of those young men was Jonathan Kay who you will get to meet in

---

• Barry was one of Jonathan's nurses who cared for him during his bone marrow transplant and in the last stages of leukaemia treatments at University College Hospital, London.

the pages of this book. No book can really capture the beauty and uniqueness of the person Jonathan was. The following pages tell the journeys of many people through the eyes and thoughts of Jonathan and his mother, Brenda. Other people will come in and out of the story, reminding us that cancer affects not just the sufferer. None of us can afford to be just onlookers.

Jonathan's words are often humorous, sometimes sad, sometimes angry, but they are always human. They especially challenge us to think about how we treat those who become ill. A noted researcher describes the nurse as a 'skilled companion', claiming that as nurses we are to be companions to those we care for, both patient and family alike. I would argue that no matter what role we work – doctors, chaplains, friends, therapists, family or nurses – we are all called to be 'skilled companions'. Jonathan's words unfortunately tell us that at times we have not always fulfilled that role well.

A word on Jonathan's particular illness. In ALL, cells that normally protect and strengthen the body develop abnormally. These cells are described as immature because they have been unable to develop into the healthy cells they are suppose to be. Multiplying at an abnormal rate these immature cells prevent healthy cells from forming. Instead of fulfilling their protective function they leave the body vulnerable to multiple infections and problems. It is potentially fatal.

In the early pages of his journals, Jonathan talks of the recurring infections that never seem to go away and the onset of pain, symptoms of the presence of these numerous abnormal cells. A simple blood test revealed that Jonathan's immature cell counts were abnormally high, and further tests confirmed his diagnosis. Jonathan describes his own treatment in the pages to follow, the weeks and months of being confined to hospital for multiple tests and treatments, the relief at getting home for a few days. He vividly describes how his life changed in the light of his diagnosis, a story familiar to anyone who has experienced cancer.

Reading his diary I was struck that as Jonathan was celebrating Millennium night with his friends on the banks of the river Thames, I was less than a mile away working night duty with a friend. Having got through his year of treatment for Leukaemia, Jonathan was enjoying life like the rest of us. A few months later he relapsed. Later that year we would meet for the first time and so we became part of each other's story.

I worked as a nurse on the ward where Jonathan had come to receive a bone marrow transplant from his brother Thomas. Jonathan's treatment involved receiving high doses of chemotherapy drugs and intensive radiation treatment known as Total Body Irradiation (TBI). These treatments have two aims: (1) to remove any remaining cancer cells that exist in the body; and (2) to destroy the person's existing immune system. Having achieved these aims, the patient is transplanted with bone marrow from a donor with a closely matched blood type, which enables a new immune system to develop free of any cancer cells.

Many difficulties can occur during the transplant process: damage and side effects can occur as a result of the chemotherapy and radiation; the new transplanted immune system may not develop; or ironically it may attack the recipient or the cancer cells may return. In Jonathan's case the transplant was temporarily successful. He was able to develop a new immune system with his brother's bone marrow, but unfortunately his cancer returned within a short period of time. In an attempt to slow down his advancing disease Jonathan was given more chemotherapy, but without success.

I remember the first time I met Jonathan, or maybe I should say I remember the first time I heard about Jonathan. I had come on to the ward to begin an afternoon shift. My colleague explaining the plan of care for the ward described how a young man with ALL had been admitted to the ward to begin treatment for a transplant, and already he was proving to be difficult. Sometimes the word 'difficult' is used to describe a patient who is not afraid to say what he/she needs and wants, even when it does not fit into the existing health care system. I must confess on entering his room I did feel a little nervous, wondering what to expect. Jonathan was reading a newspaper, and his mum Brenda was sitting quietly reading a book. That was a scene that I was to witness many times over the next months: mother and son sitting together walking and journeying a difficult path.

Throughout his treatment Jonathan kept a diary. His thoughts and reflections give a glimpse of the person he was, not just a man with cancer but a man with a life to live. I remember hearing a friend of Jonathan's read a piece from his diary after his death, when Jonathan describes crying himself to sleep, something he felt he needed to do as a form of catharsis. I found that difficult because I myself had never seen him cry, reminding me that even nurses often do not see or hear the full story. Jonathan describes the loneliness and the isolation he feels, separated from his friends as he spends his days dealing with his treatment. The same treatment that continually forces Jonathan to meet a multitude of strangers some who sometimes become friends or confidantes.

His funeral again reminded me that I had only got a glimpse of who he really was. I had to smile when one of his friends on meeting me said, 'Oh you must be the nurse that Jonathan made the tape of music for.' I smiled, because although Jonathan and I chatted about many things, our views on music were, shall we say, miles apart. Jonathan followed Punk. I'm a bit of a Barbra Streisand fan.

I remember a day laughing with Jonathan and his mum when it dawned on me that I was closer in age to Brenda than I was to Jonathan, showing just how the truth can hurt. Laughter is an important part of Jonathan's story. I recall when I once told Jonathan that I had thought he was a Conservative supporter. I was wrong, to put it mildly. As I left the room I could see the concerned look on Jonathan's face, as if to say 'If that guy can make that kind of mistake, is he really capable of looking after me?' I think he forgave me a few days later.

Rarely did I see Jonathan without a morning paper, a book, talking on the phone or fiddling with his laptop. These rituals always took priority over his so-called 'important' clinical tasks. We talked of many things: the affairs of the world, his frustration with the health care system, his hopes, and eventually the reality that he was dying. I enjoyed the company of Jonathan and Brenda. I like to think that I was able to journey with them a while.

Today I continue to care for patients with leukaemia, and I also help to educate health care professionals who wish to specialise in the field of cancer. With Brenda's permission, I have used Jonathan's words to help give an insight into the story of a person living with cancer. I particularly like Jonathan's reflection of 'The Hill' and his analogy of riding his bike. I encourage the professionals I teach to really listen to the stories each patient has to share – not just to record on an assessment chart, but to learn. While it is obviously vital that we continue to look into the causes of leukaemia and to continue to develop even more treatments, they can only be carried out against a background of listening to the stories people tell, stories like the one you are about to read.

I liked Jonathan. Yes, I liked him. Why? Maybe because he was a young man who was in charge of his own care. He demanded to be involved.

And he spoke honestly about the fact that he was dying. I remember shortly before he was transferred out of ITU for the last time, I asked him how he felt. He told me he was not afraid to die, just sad that he was not going to get to do the things he wanted to do.

Norbert Elias in his book *The Loneliness of the Dying*† says that we are in danger of pushing the dying away from us, separating them from the rest of society. Until we begin to challenge the notion that death is not supposed to happen, until we begin to accept death and dare I say celebrate it, then Elias's words will remain true. I believe we live in a society that overvalues productivity, and therefore the ill and the elderly who appear to be no longer productive can be pushed aside. People like Jonathan will not allow that to happen. He forces us to listen. I don't think Jonathan wanted to die, of course, but he died in the presence of two wonderful people, his parents Peter and Brenda, who loved him, along with an extended group of family and friends who did the same.

In the following pages Jonathan describes his journey with leukaemia and the treatments it demanded. Every now and again (in the italicised sections) you will hear the voice of his mother Brenda share what it was like for her and the family. Time and time again Brenda talks of the need for staff to treat Jonathan as an adult who wanted to know what was going on. Jonathan was no fool. Brenda continually allowed Jonathan to take the leading role even when at times it was difficult for her to remain silent. Brenda stayed with Jonathan throughout his treatment, and it was a relationship that worked. Sometimes I would go into the room to find Brenda and Jonathan sitting quietly, and I could tell by body language that cross words had been spoken. I might return a short time later and the body language told me that a reconciliation had occurred. Brenda's words vividly portray the angst and love of a mother who must care for all her sons, even while one is dying.

Jonathan spoke of the many ordinary things he wanted to do: going to a racing track and driving a fast motor car, getting another tattoo, going to a concert with his friends, visiting the United States again. Jonathan made no secret of his desire to be a journalist, and I believe he would have made a good one. He spoke of getting through his treatment and looking forward to studying for a postgraduate qualification in journalism.

---

†Elias, N. (1985) *The Loneliness of the Dying*. Continuum. London

Unfortunately, he did not get to achieve these things, but he did get to tell his story, the story you are about to read, and in doing so he has become the writer he wanted to be. I think Jonathan would be pleased to know you are reading his work.

Barry Quinn
January 2005

THE STORY SO FAR...

Warning: if you are someone who knows me, you've probably heard this more than once. It is undoubtedly even less amusing and/or interesting upon subsequent exposure.

TUESDAY 18TH AUGUST 1998
Work, my least favourite pastime. My simple-enough job at Transcare Distribution, Leicester, takes a horrid turn when I develop stabbing pains in my back. I put it down to the cheap office chairs and inappropriate desk height. As I drive home the pain worsens, and I vow to see the doctor the next day.

WEDNESDAY 19TH AUGUST 1998
See the GP (not my regular) in my parental hometown of Grantham. I apparently have appalling posture, am too tall for chairs, desks etc. (I'm 6'3"), and could do with loosing a little weight. I am given a set of exercises to do which I duly follow.

Am advised to quit my job. I provide little argument against this.

THURSDAY 20TH AUGUST 1998
My employers seem less than convinced as I only had 2 days left on my contract. I am no longer in their good books, it appears. No job however is worth risking your health. Not for £5 an hour on a night shift, it isn't.

THURSDAY 27TH AUGUST–SUNDAY 30TH AUGUST 1998
After a week of being a good boy scout and performing my exercises, my back seems significantly better. I set off for the Guardian Television and Young People' conference /weekend affair in Edinburgh. This weekend is insane and has quite a few stories of its own, but I digress... I return home thoroughly exhausted.

MONDAY 31ST AUGUST 1998

I hook up with two buddies of mine from sunny California – Mike and Chris[1]. We're going to be taking them to see the sights for a few days. Anyone who followed the Dagobah US tour will know them as two solid, upstanding types, indeed Mike organised the whole thing. Somehow, I'm still exhausted from Edinburgh and have developed a flu[2], but I just put this down to lack of sleep. Rest is not an option though as we have to show these guys what the UK has to offer!

(Note to all you cynical punk rock types: show foreigners around your country of origin for a while, and you WILL begin to notice all the benefits we take for granted.)

TUESDAY 1ST SEPTEMBER–THURSDAY 3RD SEPTEMBER 1998

Phew – Indian food, ten pin bowling, alcohol, Sherwood Forest, Ice cream, Alton Towers, beer, food, Leicester, Grantham, special Dagobah gig with Americans as guest vocalists, I get sick, I get better, other people get sick – is there a bug going round? Off to Paris, where nothing of note manages to happen...

TUESDAY 8TH SEPTEMBER 1998

Dum da-da Dum! The sword of Damocles drops and manages to work its way down to my lower back. We're in London (I'm so fucking cosmopolitan, I know)[3]. We're in a very pleasant hostel by Finsbury Park, but it's already early evening so we head on out for entertainment in Camden. Food is priority one. Some rather nice falafel later, and we hit Camden town. It was an easy punch; Camden is pretty fucking dead (we forgot that it's out of term time).

We go to a few pubs and then strange things happen. We're in Bar Risa and my stomach, back, and head all decide to go um-bongo on me. The guys all want to go on to a club which is fair enough, so I make my apologies and catch a black cab back to the hostel. I retire to bed.

Now, I'm no hard man, but I know what it feels like to break a bone or to have a severe asthma attack. That night was the most painful of my life.

---

1 Mike Woodburn and Chris Jacques are two friends of Jonathan's from California.
2 'Flu' can be a sign of an immune system not working properly.
3 In this entry, Jonathan has been travelling with friends, Mike, Chris, Tony and Andy.

I'm passing out then being re-awakened by waves of agony that crash against every bone and muscle in my body. I suffocate as my lungs seize up and my back is pulled apart. Not good.

Putting on my clothes nearly kills me. By this time tears are pouring from my eyes as the itchy feel of sweat plasters my hair to my scalp and causes a burning sensation when I move. It's like climbing a mountain backwards, but I triumphantly make the five flights of stairs to the lobby. There's a business type at the desk talking to the receptionist about a wake-up call or something. I feel I deserve priority:

Me:	'I need to get to a hospital, NOW!'
Business-type:	'You'll have to wait in line.' (turning to the original customer) 'Now, sir, when would you like your wake-up call?'
Original customer: '	About 7.30 I think, but will I be able to get breakfast?'

This lowers my faith in humanity. Not only do the staff ignore desperate cries for medical attention, but the customer considers the agony of a fellow customer to be a rude inconvenience! There is no hope for this world. I can now fully understand the hermitic, the homicidal and the misanthropic. Contemplation upon the more sociopathic elements of human existence soon gives way to pain and exhaustion, and I collapse across the lobby seating. Some time later the receptionist calls over:

Receptionist:	'So you want a hospital?'
Me:	'Yes please.'
Receptionist:	'Where is nearest hospital?' (sic)
Me:	'I don't know! Call 999 or something!'

The receptionist calls his mate (or his dad possibly, I'm not sure) who arrives in the lobby. He asks me some stuff, I think mainly to check I'm not just some piss artist. So finally a minicab gets called, and I'm off to Hackney hospital.

The hospital is pleasant enough I guess, some nicely strong painkillers certainly help pass the time, and it's 2am by the time I'm awake again. To cut an already far too long story short, the doctor gives me some painkillers for my back and recommends I see my GP in case there are any other more serious concerns to be examined.

Postscript – I returned to the hostel to find my companions asleep. The receptionist provided them with the following info as they checked in: 'Your mate has gone to hospital.' That's it. Luckily their own resources enabled them to call the hospital through a process of geographically based elimination until they could confirm I was OK. That receptionist is going to go far...

WEDNESDAY SEPTEMBER 9TH 1998

So little time and so much crap to espouse! OK, so the next day we have a laugh about the previous night's proceedings and lie in a bit. Eventually, mid-afternoon, we show our transatlantic guests some 'tourist shit'. As none of us have ever been, the London Dungeon seems an obvious place (and of course for the Misfits connotations). It's quite cool really but my back's beginning to hurt. We head to Leicester Square and go to Planet Hollywood (how English!). It's nothing to write home about, so it's certainly nothing to write to you about. OK then, I'll indulge my restaurant critic fantasies: Food is bland, service is saccharine sweet and over-efficient, but damn the Ghostbusters Proton Pack is cool. I'm tired and aching now, so I make my apologies and head home for some rest.

FRIDAY SEPTEMBER 11TH 1998

After a much needed day of rest, (I slept for 20 hours!) I travel to Cambridge for our final night out before Mike and Chris return to California and Tony and Celene[4] go on holiday to NYC. I'm due to take them all to Gatwick in the morning. We have a cool night out but go to bed early due to rigorous travelling schedules the next day. I am not well at bedtime, but I try and ride it out.

SATURDAY SEPTEMBER 12TH 1998

Urgh. I get through the airport bit OK, but I'm feeling decidedly rough on the journey home. Not much to say other than I slept and felt ill a lot (at home that is, not in the car). I make an appointment to see my GP in Grantham on Monday.

SUNDAY SEPTEMBER 13TH 1998

I am in a bad, bad way. Mid afternoon it becomes clear that I am not going to be safe to travel the treacherous 30 miles of the A607 to Grantham tomorrow. I call my folks and ask them to pick me up this afternoon. They come and get me around 4pm, and then I relax until the evening,

4 Tony's then-girlfriend, now wife.

when everything changed...

So, to set the scene – a thought occurs. When does a scene require 'setting'? The events that relate to my illness and its onset pertain to me and a mutation of my bone marrow cells, the physical environment is of little or no consequence. Had my illness been spawn nucleic, as the result of over-exposure to benzene or a childhood spent living next to a plant manufacturing uranium encased shells for the Gulf War then yes, perhaps a scene would need to be set. However, it will have to suffice to say that the unexplained causes of Acute Lymphoblastic Leukaemia attained their 'acute' nature (in terms of sensation) at around 9.30 pm on the above date in the bedroom of my teenage youth in my parental home whilst attempting to watch *Schindler's List* (and I have the gall to discuss suffering! Since when did my name become Primo Levi?) for the second or third time.

Enough moral posturing. Time has now moved to several hours later as I squirm on a hospital bed in the Accident and Emergency department of Grantham general hospital. A friendly doctor takes charge. I forget his name, my mum has it written[5] down, but he is the closest figure to which I can credit the identification of my maladies as being marginally more life threatening than a sore back and a cold. A blood test, urine test, chest X-ray and ECG (Electro-Cardio-Graph) all follow but the results to my layman's eye are all but nonsensical. In particular the chest X-ray revealed, at least to me if not the apothecaries, that I am missing six ribs whilst enjoying the benefits of having a small plastic skull lodged inside my left lung. Call me paranoid, but the pseudo-scientific gobbledegook did little to convince me otherwise (as if my heart looks like that!).

Note to self: I use too many brackets. I will attempt to do so less in the future. For now, my apologies.

Cynicism, medical paranoia and self-defeating literary criticism aside – the medical practitioners' insistence upon these exciting and expensive tests do imbue one with a certain sense of self importance. This diverts one's attention from both the pain and, with the benefit of hindsight, the blindingly obvious logic that the more expensive and exciting the test, the more serious and complicated the illness. My conclusion? The taxpayer's wallet is a greater anaesthetic than morphine, chloroform or even the delightful DF118's[6] that I munch my way through on a daily basis.

5 Dr Wilson.
6 Dihydrocodeine, a strong pain reliever.

Anyway, my pain and anxiety are soon brought to an end by the slightly worrying, but not entirely heart stopping news that my platelet count is low. For those of us who didn't take GCSE biology, they're the things that allow your blood to clot and form scabs. A normal count is around 150[7] or so, mine was 32. And after this lengthy examination was brought to a close by this diagnosis and a prescription for further observation, I shall bring this increasingly verbose and convoluted entry to a literal euthanasia via the grammatically lethal injection of a full stop.

SUNDAY SEPTEMBER 13TH 1998

A normal Sunday afternoon and the only decision to be made is whether to watch East Enders or have a nap. But then the phone rings. It's Jonathan, obviously in a great deal of pain and rather distressed. This is so out of character that we leave for Leicester immediately to pick him up.

When we arrive home, he settles down on the settee and seems much calmer. An appointment is already arranged with the GP for the following day, so there appears to be very little more that we can do. Peter and I go out dancing, but I am unable to enjoy myself. Call it a mother's instinct, but I insist we return home early.

Jonathan is waiting for us at the door; he is pacing up and down, distraught with pain. A&E seems the best option, so we set out for the local hospital.

It's 10 pm by now. We are seen almost immediately. They start asking Jonathan question after question, many of them very personal: 'When did you last have sex?' 'Are you gay?' 'Where did you get this tattoo?'[8] I offer to leave to give him some privacy but Jonathan asks me to stay.

He's obviously worried and so am I; this is clearly not just backache.

The clock ticks by slowly. More questions, blood tests, an ECG and an x-ray. The medical registrar has been sent for. All this at 2am on a Monday morning. Alarm bells ring in my head, but outwardly I remain calm, reassuring Jonathan that 'the doctor's just being thorough'. Who's kidding who here? We both know it's something serious but nobody wants to say

---

7 Jonathan is actually incorrect; a normal platelet count is between 300-400, so his was even more serious than he understood.

8 The rationale behind these questions is that doctors have spotted Jonathan's immune system not functioning properly, and they would like to rule out HIV.

it out loud.

At 4am I finally leave. Jonathan has been found a bed and will be admitted. I go home and try to sleep. It's a restless night, spoiled by scenarios from all the different TV hospital dramas that I now realise I've spent too much time watching.

MONDAY 14TH SEPTEMBER 1998

Well, that's my first night in a hospital over. Jesus this 'how it started thing' was supposed to be a couple of paragraphs long. I sure hope you're finding it interesting – if not, haven't you got anything better to do than read thousands of words of text which you don't find at all stimulating? Different strokes I guess.

If you've been in a hospital you know what the deal is anyway: They steal your blood, you throw up on them, you ignore the food they spend hours preparing whilst you lie around in your pants all day. I could joke that this is like living with my parents, but I feel that the obvious-joke fairy would hit me with her crap humour stick.

TUESDAY 15TH SEPTEMBER 1998

Today I noticed for the first time my uncanny transformation into a smack addict. I am unshaven and my face is battered and bruised (due to the lack of platelets in my blood)[9]. I have tracks up my arms where blood has been taken and I sleep all day, able only to slur incomprehensibly at the few visitors who have the misfortune to peak round my door.

The staff feel further investigation is required so they have me transferred to Pilgrim Hospital, Boston. Unfortunately that's Boston, Lincolnshire, not Boston Massachusetts, so don't contact me asking for cheap Taang! Records products. I get a nice ambulance drive over there, and I talk computers with one of the medics, which is nice. I get my own funky little room at Boston, which I must say is nicer then the hotel that I recently stayed in Paris, obviously a lot cheaper and with a hospital stuck on the end of it. Brilliant! Just the place for a vacation if you have a hideous illness. Actually I have the separate room to stop my weakened immune system being exploited by all the hideous diseases hanging around in the wards. Tip- if you're gonna go into hospital, get those white blood cells

---

9 Platelets aid in clotting, and therefore bruising is far more likely when platelet counts are low.

low to ensure you get the Presidential suite.

If this also sounding rather jocular then bear in mind that two new phrases entered my life today: Hodgkin's Disease and Leukaemia. Unfortunately the commercial break came up and we had to wait to find out whether I would win the star prize.

WEDNESDAY 16TH SEPTEMBER 1998
I am actually writing this next week's entries a week after the fact (artist's prerogative), and it has just struck me that I have lived with the consequences of this day for an entire week now and that it has probably had a more profound effect on my life than any other consecutive string of seven 24 hour periods. You know the end result, but the day I guess provides some interest. I'm gonna write about it anyway, so for a mildly entertaining anti-climax read on.

One incident I neglected to mention earlier was that upon commencing my stay at Boston, I had a 'cannula' inserted into my left forearm. This is the needle part of the intravenous drip that allows both the insertion of fluid into my veins and the removal of blood cultures. At various points this has been relocated to the back of my left hand and then the back of my right hand. It is an awkward adornment for any manipulative part of one's body and its main impracticality (in a purely aesthetic and locomotive sense of course) is its attachment by a thin plastic cable to a huge metal stand with the drip bags and tubes attached to it. Just like in Carry on Matron.

What is perhaps less well known is that the pump which forces the saline solution (for example) into one's vein has a short battery life, so consequently spends its time attached to the wall by means of 3 metre power cable. The line from the pump to the vein is 1 metre. This gives me an area of mobility equivalent to a 4 metre radius semicircle centred at the nearest power point. This effectively means that you just don't leave your room. It's a good thing I've lost my appetite as well because having a regular crap would be impossible. Apologies for such crudities when discussing medical science, but a man observes such things. I'm moaning, I'm sure many of you have experienced IV drips before, so I'd better stop showing off, haven't I?

Where were we? Ah, yes. So anyway last night I didn't tell my mum the real possibilities of what I was facing. I used vague terms like 'viral infection' and allowed my Dad, who was with me at the time, to tell her alone in private last night. They come in, with my three younger brothers, to see me in the evening, and of course to hopefully find out what I actually have. So to continue the other crap gameshow analogy- By the way please don't expect any Swift-like misanthropy, or cutting social conjecture upon man's fascination with the failure and fortune of others as a means of entertainment. I just get bored of being so literal.

UNKNOWN TO OUR CONTESTANT JON... A last minute booby (well, star prize) has been added: behind Door Number One is a particularly nasty case of Glandular Fever which can be treated with a course of antibiotics; Door Number Two hides the rather tricky but ultimately treatable Hodgkin's Disease, again with a course of antibiotics, a hospital stay, but the opportunity to return to University without any significant interruption to my studies; finally Door Number Three with Bully's special prize: Acute Lymphoblastic Leukaemia. Yes, that's right, identical-looking but completely useless white blood cells are formed in the bone marrow which then overflow into the blood killing all the good cells, rendering your immune system useless. The prize comes with 6 months of chemotherapy, antibiotics and of course a complete bone marrow transplant!'

Unfortunately saying that I have had a great time and would like to go home happy with what I have so far would not only be a lie, but completely impossible. In lieu of their superior expertise I allow the doctors to choose.

'Door Number Three,' say the doctors.

'Acute Lymphoblastic Leukaemia is a disease normally found in children, but can occur in younger adults as well. In addition to the symptoms and medication described above our lucky winner will also endure complete hair loss, probable infertility, continual muscular pains, an uncomfortably enlarged liver and spleen, sickness, loss of appetite, regular vomiting, dehydration, tiredness, inability to sleep for normal periods of time, loss of an entire academic year and/or the ability to take up employment, the status granted by the title 'cancer victim', constipation, the need for medical checkups for several years, an intolerance to all other diseases and of course the knowledge that 91% of the cells in your bone marrow are cancerous! And who could forget the ever present risk of premature death?'

'Oh.'

THURSDAY 17TH SEPTEMBER 1998
My first day in the trenches of My War! Boot camp is over and my life as a front line cancer victim begins! I am surprisingly (to myself) ambivalent regarding the whole affair. The sense of novelty and excitement are still there as well as the acute awareness that one has become the nucleus of one's social atom. Friends and family swarm like protons and electrons with inevitable collisions which result primarily from future concern for the decaying core. If all this sounds rather micro-nihilistic then perhaps I am failing to convey the sheer production of energy that this reaction affords. My friends and family have become mobilised to the reactionary agent with only the most benevolent of motives.

Perhaps this would be an appropriate juncture to extend my heartfelt thanks to all those who have provided me with the appropriate energies to maintain my current sense of well being. It amazes me when I am told 'it's fabulous how you manage to keep such a positive attitude about this, you're so brave,' without realising that this is the expression of genuine concern and the exclusion of the negativity and sombre pontification that both ignite and catalyse my so called 'positive outlook'. I am all too aware that this particular paragraph is descending into a quagmire of lexical masturbation so I'll keep it simple: Thanks to everyone – you will never know how much it means to me.

I think I'll leave it at that for today. I had some injections and stuff.

FRIDAY 18TH SEPTEMBER 1998
Ironic that I should describe yesterday's notes as being akin to masturbation, for the metaphorical transcends into the literal today. The doctors say that I'm being transferred to Nottingham in order to cryogenically store a sample of my sperm in order to allow for post-chemotherapy fertilisation to induce the pregnancy of a human child inside the womb of the mother of that future human child. To me it seems easier to think that my Dad is giving me a lift down the road to wank into a jar inside a public toilet. That is, I'm afraid, the glamour of sperm donation. An awkwardly attractive doctor talks to you for ten minutes, furnishes you with a selection of cheap British porno mags from the late 1980's and provides the use of a locked lavatory in order to 'produce a sample'. I've been throwing up for the best part of the day and only want to sleep. I peruse the pornography only to be distracted by the interview with Shawn Kemp (former Seattle Sonics power forward) inside a rather awkward looking copy of Penthouse USA edition. The interview seems a little embarrassed to be included alongside the readers' wives fare. After forty minutes of feeling

sick, sleepy and unaroused, I decided to give it a miss today. In case any-one didn't pick up on this earlier, the treatment I am receiving may make me infertile, so this whole process is a bit of a 'rainy day' policy, but on a childbirth tip.

FRIDAY 18TH SEPTEMBER
Where do I begin? The last few days seem so unreal. I have continued working because what else can you do if you want to pretend life is still normal?

On Tuesday evening, I find myself staring at an episode of East Enders. It is at this point, of all points, that my husband tells me the doctors are think-ing that Jonathan may have leukaemia. I am unable to speak. Tears stream silently down my face. Peter continues that the thing that concerns Jonathan the most is how I will take the news. Me, he is worried about me. Oh, son, why?

A new phase in our lives begins. All too soon the long winding fog-bound A52 to Boston becomes drearily familiar. Even when you arrive the hospi-tal is at the other side of the town. Door to door the average journey time is a good 55 minutes, a long time to try not to think about anything. We're lucky we have a car; like the rest of non-urban England, the journey by public transport is an absolute farce. On our first visit, we park the car and, with great difficulty, pay the fee. When you're in a state of great emotion-al stress the last thing you need is finding bloody change to park your car.

I am totally amazed by the profusion of cigarette butts around the entrance to the ward, most of which are being produced by patients getting a quick nicotine fix. Who am I to criticise? My chocolate consumption rate has more than doubled this week. We enter the ward. The smell of stale cooked food lingers in the air; cabbage and cauliflower may have been on tonight.

We get to Jonathan's room. We exchange greetings then just stare at each other. What do you say? Denton (the doctor) enters. He has a happy smile on his face, which is unnerving. He stands legs together, almost jumping up and down he is so keen to communicate his findings with us. His cheery dis-position gives me a feeling of dread. This must be the lead up to bad news. He gives out a great deal of information. There is a new vocabulary to learn. My brain only takes in the words cancer, leukaemia and POSSIBLE treatment. Suddenly, Denton notices Jonathan's three younger brothers. He almost leaps into the air. More new words enter the conversation:

sibling, transplant, success possibilities are the order of the day.

We are all quiet on the drive back. We have no desire to state the obvious and upset one another.

SATURDAY 19TH SEPTEMBER 1998

Basically a repeat command wanking performance. The antibiotics (or is it the morphine?) are making me sick, and I puke all the way to the hospital. Another no-show – I'm just too ill. It turns out the strong fertility record of my family means that I probably wont be that badly affected anyhow. I'll still be able to have kids someday, and that's good enough for me – I'm in no rush. Oh dear, I think hyphens are becoming my new brackets – I must be cautious.

My folks have been buying me loads of cool toys like a Gameboy and a VCR. Parents rule. Basically apart from the fact that I'm hideously ill, patient life is pretty bounteous.

SUNDAY 20TH SEPTEMBER 1998

Fairly lazy day today. Just relaxed after the trauma of the last few days. Had some visitors. I'm not gonna go name checking throughout this text. If you visited me you know it, if you didn't you probably don't know me, and I doubt you'd care anyway. Visitors are nice though. If you know someone who's ill or depressed then go visit. It does more for one's happiness and recovery than any of the drugs or treatments. I should write counselling pamphlets or something.

MONDAY 21ST SEPTEMBER 1998

Not the most pleasant of days as far as my treatment is concerned and not just for myself. In order to find a suitable donor for my bone-marrow transplant, my brothers (three younger, remember?) are brought in for blood tests. Bets are already being placed by medical staff, family and friends as to who is the most likely. For some reason the hot favourite is my youngest brother, Thomas. They spend the morning having sharp objects stuck in their arms, then are informed the results will take 10 days.

Meanwhile the hero of the story is busy facing up to the daunting task of drinking an entire litre and a half of orange squash which has been laced with cellular dye. The catch? The dye makes it taste of liquorice, and I fucking hate the stuff. But why? Ah, well, I'm having a CT scan so the Docs can play spot the cancer cells (it can't be that hard, they said 91% of the cells were bad 'uns). The dye attaches to the cells then glows under the

CT scan. The big circular tube thing that looks like a Star Trek prop, that's the thing.

I manage about two small glasses of squash in the waiting room of the radiology department, then throw up into their rather nice tissue box holder in front of a rather worried looking teenage patient with a petrified looking mum. I grin with orange sputum dripping down my chin. They go and wait somewhere else. The scan is fairly non-eventful, so I brighten up the room by puking again afterwards. The young kid from earlier doesn't want to have his scan anymore. The put me in a wheelchair and rush me off so I can be sick in a different department.

Oh you'll like this – to punish me for my puking sins, the surgeons play reverse voodoo on me in the afternoon. Somewhere in the hospital a small woollen effigy of my corporeal form convulses and squirms as painfully real sharp objects are forced into my living flesh. It seems an odd way to take out revenge on errant children's toys, but the doctors think it's worthwhile. They remove the cannula from my left forearm and insert it in the back of my hand. This is not comfortable, so the obvious conclusion is to insert an additional cannula in the back of my right hand. I am informed that anaesthetic is, of course, for girls.

TUESDAY 22ND SEPTEMBER 1998

So they ripped them all out. Yes, all that fucking cannula business was pointless as a more permanent solution is now apparently a necessity. You see, cannulas heal over, which makes the pump stop, and I don't like be woken every ten minutes to have to restart my IV drip. It sucks. So (and this time anaesthetic, though just local, is permitted) a small gas main, which the doctor's call a Hickmann connection[10], is installed into my chest. A plastic tube is inserted into my flesh above my left nipple and travels around 6 inches to a 'major vein' under the collar bone (I think this is the vena cava but both my biology and my ability to remember to ask about such things fail me)[11]. It's got two taps coming out of the bottom where you can either insert drugs or remove blood. These two portals will provide the majority of access for my chemotherapy. I like my Hickmann connection a lot. Although the operation was painful (and rather boring) it is a most convenient appendage. I heartily recommend it.

---

10 A Hickmann line is like a permanent valve that allows blood and drugs to be given to a patient, as well as blood sample to be drawn, without having to constantly reinsert a hypodermic.

11 It is the vena cava; it is the primary vein returning to the heart.

WEDNESDAY 23RD SEPTEMBER 1998

YES! I have to apologise for the sketchiness of the previous week's notes because we are now back in real time! It is 11.35pm on above date, and I am no longer writing post-humously. Ironically, I appear to be slipping out of strict present tense, but fuck grammar! I'm finally on time!

So I wake up and set myself the goal of getting this column up to real time (I am aware that this phrase is not entirely accurate, but what the hey?). In order to achieve this I have breakfast with my dad, read the *Guardian* and its supplements from front to back, read 200 pages of *American Psycho* which for some reason I am compelled to begin again, even though I'm half way through a Gabriel Garcia Marquez, receive 10 guests (including my dad) and piss off the nursing staff. I apparently receive too many phone calls and clog up the network. I am asked to ask my friends to not all call at once. Of course my friends in Leeds, Brighton, London, Leicester, Tel Aviv, San Jose, Huddersfield, Cambridge, and Northampton are in regular contact with each other, and this is a breeze to sort out. A hospital representative apologises later. I am very grateful for this, as until now the staff and facilities have been amazing, and I thought we all got on fine. I hate to take advantage, but it's not my fault if people who live 3000 miles from each other decide to phone at the unbelievable time of early evening (why don't they phone at 4am like normal people?). It's sorted.

After getting a week behind, My War, as far as I am concerned is now up to date. The future beckons. The reports from now on will now include my favourite thing – my opinion, and a whole lot else to boot. In fact you've probably just finished the interesting bit. I'm now gonna turn into a regular anal columnist, but hey – I've still got that leukaemia sympathy vote up my sleeve...

IS IT LIVE?

I began this project relishing getting to the stage where I could get all the exposition out of the way and start espousing opinion as well as mere history. Suddenly, a sense of being out of one's depth is all encompassing. The curious aspect to writing opinion in this solitary mode is the perhaps unwelcome liberation it confers upon the demagogue. Unfettered by interjection or cross-examination I no longer walk a tightrope between an embarrassing outburst in a crowded bar or a well placed arrow of intuition through the dense combat of conversation, but rather have been left to explore a minefield of political and literary device, which is tailor made (perhaps subconsciously, by the traversant) toward one's own personal pitfalls.

What the fuck am I moaning about? Friends of mine will stand testament to my fervour for argument and opinion. My enemies will tell you I'm full of shit. Which is pretty much the same thing really. Onwards.

THURSDAY 25TH SEPTEMBER 1998

After all of that nonsense, I have decided there will be little in the form of 'opinion' in today's report. I am at present undergoing a cultivation – a harvest if you will – of subjects which, in my most highly opinionated belief, require my opinion. One of these will have to be 'why are the no decent synonyms for *opinion*'? Other topics will undoubtedly include 'Heavy Metal is dying, it is my duty to save it', 'Why being a punk does not make you any more informed about politics', 'Is nursing the most undervalued and consequently most punk of all professions?', 'Puff Daddy is killing hip-hop', and of course many more. This initial shortlist may appear a little muso-centric, but these themes spring to mind most easily (and this column is most likely to appear in a fanzine[12], so what the hey).

---

12 The fanzine was *Fracture*, from which many of these columns appeared.

Am I a cynic? I'd like to think not. It has just occurred to me that I'm writing a column (if one can describe this unpublished and distinctly un-column shaped assemblage of prose a column. Medium or the message situation, I guess), and the name of this column is 'My War. It seemed a good idea at the time, and I'm sure you can guess why it occurred to me. Here is a list of reasons that have led me to believe it is no longer suitable:

1) I am not the biggest Black Flag fan ever. If this (not again) column, ends up in a punk fanzine, then I may well be expected to have some encyclopaedic knowledge of said recording artists. For your information I don't even possess a copy of 'My War'. I do however like pre-Rollins Black Flag, so perhaps this endows me with enough punk kudos to entitle my column thus. On the other hand I couldn't give a fuck if some twat punk kid thinks I'm a bandwagon-jumper or something. I'm so fucking punk I'm writing a column called 'My War' on an expensive laptop listening to dance music on a portable CD player. Ha! I may well buy some expensive clothes and other consumables this week to cheer myself up. Oh the battery has run out on my pager. Doesn't matter, I'm gonna get a mobile in a few days. Fuck you.

2) Oooh that did feel ever so punk – in a capitalist, consumerist and conformist kind of way. I enjoyed that. But perhaps this is another irony of my composition's title. It is not an aggressive column (at least not intentionally). I am not at war. Who is my enemy? The cancer, I guess, could be seen as such, but it has no face, no emotion, no plan. One could even say that the cancer is just doing what it does to survive, much in the same way as mould grows on bread – not malicious but it pisses you off. Am I denying my cancer the right to reproduce itself naturally? Am I committing oncological genocide? Fuck no, I just don't want to die. I just lie around and swallow chemicals. The war rages inside me in the one place that my eyes cannot see and CNN will never get a fucking camera crew. Perhaps in retrospect it is 'My War', because it's no one else's. But wars are seldom private, and I have no urge to let my Balkan powderkeg explode into the Europe of my peers. Therefore the title of my column refers to the one thing which is of no concern to either myself or the reader. I hope this made sense, but I'm quite sure it didn't. This explanation business is reason enough to abandon this fucking title.

3) 'My War' sounds a bit too close to *Mein Kampf* (*My Struggle*, Hitler, A. – from all good bookstores).

I thought there would be more reasons than this, but a ceasefire appears to have been called. The current peace accord dictates that I shall retain the title of 'My War' on account of its snappiness, instant punk cred and the fact that I can't be bothered to change it now. Any separatist movements with better ideas or threats of splinter group violence can send their superior suggestions to the usual address attached to the incendiary device of their choice.

Today's doings
I did attempt to write the 'regular bit' a while ago, but as usual I was side tracked. Here we go...

I wake up in a foul mood today. I am convinced that the pump on my IV drip is reciting a bizarre and endless mantra: 'an old and distinguished mannequin factory, an old and distinguished mannequin factory...' This has kept me up all night and needless to say, no one else can hear it when I point it out. I am pissed off with being in hospital. All the novelty and excitement has dropped from me, and I mark this by taking my first crap in a week (morphine makes you constipated) which seems an appropriate gesture. I miss breakfast, the paper takes ages to arrive and I am now taking an obscene quantity of morning chemicals. Thankfully there are lots of steroids today. and I hope that these will pick me up.

As soon as I regain my energy I resume reading *American Psycho* which I began for the third time or so yesterday. With each subsequent reading I find the description of graphic violence more disturbing and the obsessive analysis of labels and clothing more fascinating. This appears to me to be the more unexpected progression, but I find I am racing though the book so it must be good. Will Self recommended reading the whole thing in six hours (400 pages) and in terms of total reading time, I'm well on target. I am of course advanced somewhat by my prior experiences with the novel. In case anyone was wondering, you can thank Will Self for my tendency to use an eclectic vocabulary, Brett Easton Ellis for both the narcissism and self depreciation, and Gabriel Garcia Marquez / Milan Kundera for reminding me that everything I will ever write is utter shit.

I take a break from reading as by some freak chance a phone has appeared in my room. I use the opportunity to sort out my financial situation with the bank. I guess they're concerned how I am going to pay off a £1250 student overdraft with no university qualifications and a life threatening disease. They are in fact very supportive and allow me to hold my student account and all its benefits whilst out of education. I appreciate their friendliness and support, but I can just see things going wrong when I get re-aquainted with my good friends Cash Machine, Switch and Visa.

I return to reading, and by the time my Mother arrives to have dinner I have finished *American Psycho*. Five hours reading time, I reckon, but unfortunately this does not adrenalise me enough to put on a happy face for my visitor. My Mum is in a supportive mood, however. Bizarrely, watching *Animal Hospital* with her does not cause me to throw up. A Danish and yoghurt at the canteen, and I'm all smiles again! Mum leaves, and the doctors come round. They're pleased with my progress and so weekend parole looks like it's on the cards! A weekend at my parent's house never seemed so appealing. I spend the evening reminiscing about freely available telephone calls, my own taste in decor, meals that don't occur at pre-set times, internet access, no fucking IV drips!

Hmm, something is wrong with my blood sugar level[13]. Every 20 minutes a nurse comes round and shoots a staple gun into my hand. This predictably causes bleeding which is sent for the appropriate tests. It appears to be dropping but is still too high. They tell me to avoid sweets and things for a while. I am sitting in bed staring at my veins, forcing them to be less sugary. I *will* go home this weekend!

My three favourite forms of non-sexual physical recreation: swimming for fitness, skateboarding for fun, basketball for both.

Three forms of physical recreation I am forbidden from practising whist on home leave: swimming for infection risk, skateboarding for injury risk and basketball for both.

In case you were wondering, sexual intercourse is also discouraged due to the exertion required and the many lovely infections possible. Still that wasn't very likely anyway:

> 'Hey, you're nice, what do you do for a living? Student, right?
> Or a columnist (hah!) perhaps?'
> 'Well yes, but at the moment I'm actually taking year out to
> have cancer. You know, broaden my horizons....hello?...hello?'

Lights out.

---

13 The high blood sugar level is caused by a steroid treatment used to treat Jonathan's leukaemia.

FRIDAY 26TH SEPTEMBER 1998

Today was and is a motherfucker. I'll just watch *Frasier* then I'll get back to you. I can see this one taking a while… Oh god I hate the fucking English actress on *Frasier*. Why do they let her spoil a perfectly intelligent and amiable piece of programming? Niles, however, is a stroke of genius. He is a truly great character – performed with aplomb by the actor who is not Kelsey Grammer. Not to disparage Mr Grammer's performance though. He is equally competent.

Readers may notice the similarity between this passage and the rock star biographies featured in *American Psycho*, which as you know I have just re-read. Plagiarism is a curse, and today's voracious consumption of *High Fidelity* will, I fear, bring a rash of Nick Hornby-esque literary squirming resplendent across my subsequent entries. Those of you who have not read either of these fine works are either lucky to not be appalled at my blatant but subconscious lack of originality, or you're missing out on the work of two writers worth far more of your attention than I am.

The new BMW 3 Series commercial is exactly the same as the one for the (I think) Citroen Xsara. You know, all about genes, evolution and hereditary traits – that nonsense. I have no problems with cars of either a perfunctory or luxury nature, and I have no problem with accepting advertising as an artform. However the two commercials are the same fucking idea, and this annoys me for some reason. If I worked for BMW, my ad would run 'Look we had the same idea as Citroen, but our car is a lot fucking cooler, so buy it if you can afford it.' It'd work for me. Advertising provides an morbid voyeuristic pleasure for me: I like good ads, I hate bad ads, and I am one of the many naive who believes I can discern between the two. If you believe you are one of the few who are immune, one of the discerning, then I guarantee that you most certainly are not.

So anyway. I wake up today full of sunshine, but unfortunately also full of urine. I fill one of my delightful cardboard carafes and prepare myself for the day. There are two things to be happy about today: my special friend Adi is coming to visit, having just returned from her hometown of Tel Aviv, and I am due to receive confirmation that I can indeed leave this dismal place to return to somewhere slightly less dismal. In accordance with this momentous occasion I clean myself thoroughly, though avoiding the use of the shower as the force rips the dressing from my Hickmann line with a not inconsiderable degree of discomfort. This forces one to wash oneself in much the same way as one would go about doing the dishes – damp cloth and washing bowl. Washing my hair is problematic, and I am glad that I have chemotherapy as an excuse to shave it all off again. I give washing a go and feel better for a shave of my half-hearted beard.

So something had to go shit didn't it? I forget the chronology, so I'll deal with the least medical first. My friend Len calls to ask how I am, we chat and have a good laugh, but the mood turns sour as it transpires that a package sent to me as a surprise has not arrived. Enquiries at the hospital prove fruitless, and it soon becomes apparent that good old Royal Mail have nicely disposed of a selection of gifts – letters, tapes, reading material etc. These items are obviously unsuitable for a recovering cancer patient. I am annoyed about this, but the provision of a postcard from Tony and Celene in NYC does provide some consolation. They don't know about my illness yet, and I'm anticipating the post holiday catch up. 'Well actually I did keep myself busy whilst you were away...' Should be interesting. I am however slightly jealous as I love New York, and a return visit does not appear to be a realistic possibility any time soon. Ah, well.

Friday lunchtime provides the big debriefing from the doctors to the patients on the nature of their progress. I am eagerly awaiting my all clear to go home and a commendation on my excellent recovery. This, however, is not the case. The logic of this is astounding – try and keep up:

Chemotherapy affects all the cells in your body. It kills both cancerous and normal cells in order to cleanse the body of the illness and cultivate the development of healthy new cells. My response to the chemotherapy has been positive. The doctors know this because I have a very low cell count – lots of cells have died. For this reason I cannot leave the hospital as I am now extra-susceptible to infection and must await the growth of new healthy cells[14]. Paradoxically, if I had not responded to chemo, then there would be no apparent change in the composition of my blood and therefore I would be in an acceptable state of health to be discharged. The message – get well and you stay in hospital, stay ill and you get to go home. I am overwhelmed by the feeling that logic and reason are the deadliest diseases in the history of mankind. Together they must be responsible for more misery and suffering than Ebola and Lassa fever put together.

---

14 Jonathan is describing neutropaenia. Neutrophils are one of the body's white blood cells. When they are low a person is at risk of picking up infections, and therefore Jonathan must be kept away from any potential risk.

The result of all this is that I am thoroughly dejected and dismayed. A mournful look at the phone brings no respite as it lies silent, and I am left with the possibility of another fucking week here. Then Adi calls and I have to agree that five hours on the train for a twenty minute visit is a bit ridiculous after a 2am plane flight, so I return to my solitude. As is the norm with such things, I throw my face in the word blender by reading. As reported, I start *High Fidelity* around 2pm and finish it around 7pm. I enjoy it and the subject matter (communication within and expectations of relationships) seems strangely allegorical to my present situation. One of the younger doctors, I forget his title and surname, notices my mood during the afternoon and comes to cheer me up. He's of Mediterranean extraction, and I don't really get his jokes or understand his accent, but I'm comforted somewhat by his attempts at lifting my spirits. I mark him as a good man. His name escapes me. I'm not very good with names. Ah! The nurse who just came to check one me says his name is Antonio. Antonio is good man. Good people can make a difference to one's day.

But then again a lot of things can make a difference, and having continual phone grief is one of them. Oh, *South Park*'s on. I'll be back.

OK that was entertaining enough, now where was I... Oh yeah, so again the phone is fucked up, and I have incredible difficulty arranging anything for tomorrow, particularly when a nurse informs me that the consultant has said I can go home, which is in direct contravention of everything that was said earlier and OH GOD I don't know what I want to hear anymore. I want straight answers, telephones that work, and crucially, people who pick up on the other end. I make vague plans and stuff, but all the time the nurses are trying to give me a blood transfusion, and I'm coming across like some rock star who's just like 'too busy' for all this shit. I just want the night to be over, but I keep getting asked questions and people keep taking my temperature and I know its all for the best but uhhhhhh-hhhh. It dawns on me that I'm having a blood transfusion right now, and all though its not nearly as dramatic as I might have been led to expect, its still something that the Jehovah's Witnesses consider to be serious enough to be in defiance of God's will. Why this concerns me I am uncertain as the end result is just the same as an IV drip – I can't wear a shirt and its awkward to take a piss.

It's nearly midnight, but I'm hungry and not tired, yet I just want to sleep and get the whole fucking thing over so I can do it again in the morning and get through side B of this broken record. And all the time as I'm typing this I'm reminded of the last line of *American Psycho*, of which I have talked too much already, and am no doubt sickening you with, but here it is, and please indulge my (for once acknowledged) plagiarism once more:

> '...and this is followed by a sigh, then a slight shrug, then another sigh, and above one of the doors covered by velvet drapes in Harry's is a sign and on the sign in letters that match the drapes' colour are the words THIS IS NOT AN EXIT.'

And yes I am perfectly aware that this was also the title to the recent South Bank Show retrospective of Ellis. Fuck you, this is my exit, I turn off here.

SATURDAY 27TH SEPTEMBER 1998

A rather diminutive entry today I feel,. It's really too late for me to be doing this, but 'My War' has become at best a passion but at worst a compulsion, so urges of some kind must be fulfilled, even for only the quickest of fixes. I wake up today (a good sign) and am immediately thrust into a maelstrom of confused visitors, rapid blood transfusions (again) and helpful but omnipresent medical staff. It all makes for a very tiring day, but unfortunately one devoid of any real content suitable for my effort or your attention. I did finally manage to make it home. I'm using my desktop now, but the keyboard appears to offer no advantage to my outrageous typing. I simply must get to bed. Sorry about this, but things went OK today, and sometimes that's the most distressing and tiring situation of all. I've got my bedroom set up, my vinyl back within my grasp, and a Hunter S. Thompson size bag of drugs on the table in front of me. Admittedly prescription makes for less interesting reading than hedonism, so go read *Fear and Loathing in Las Vegas* in the meantime, okay? You should be doing this anyway, what with the impending cinematic release. Oh fuck why can't I escape talking about novels you've either already read or don't care about anyway? Urgh. I promise to write something interesting tomorrow.

SUNDAY 27TH SEPTEMBER 1998

Cheating somewhat, it's actually Monday, but I don't want any blank entries. My relaxing weekend at home was more tiring than any course of chemo, so I'm afraid yesterday's (being today's as you read it) didn't get done. A warning – Microsoft Word 97 is not backwards compatible with Word 6. It reckons it can save files in Word 6 format, but it's bollocks, especially if you're talking Win 3.x and Win 95 versions. My advice stick to .rtf format, its the only safe way when moving between versions. The whole thing pissed me off so much that I couldn't face either of my computers (my babies!) back at my folk's house, so I decided to wait until I'd calmed down and write this on the morning after as some sort of tech-no-hangover cure.

Sunday was a good day though. I finally got my knick knacks organised at my parents' house. I must confess to being an organisation streak. I love setting up my room the way I like, getting the stereo plugged in (always first priority), organising my books and things. Homemaker masochism even slips in when I admit to myself the challenge of making the speaker wires stretch far enough or positioning the scanner for easy access, despite the restrictions sanctioned by a serial access cable. I OD'd when I had both the laptop and desktop running simultaneously, and this is the rea-son for the problems described above. A further complication was that I neglected to take 12 steroid pills (made by Pfizer, of Viagra fame) at tea time, so I ended up taking them in the evening. This meant I spent the night eating when I should have been sleeping[15]. And this brings us to:

MONDAY 28TH SEPTEMBER 1998

6.30 am, my Dad wakes me, though I've only been sleeping for about three hours. I can steel feel the dull buzz of the steroids. Like a true junkie I tuck into my Gonzo bag and neutralise any suggestions of slumber with a good healthy dose of Pfizer's finest. Add to this a few other brightly coloured cylinders and a couple of powdery white discs and it's time for breakfast.

The journey to hospital is uneventful enough, but I still can't help but rabbit on about Sony Minidisc! My dad must be so bored of it now, but I have developed an unhealthy fetish for the things. At least it means we can ignore the dire nonsense that Zoe Ball is spouting this morning. I resolve to present the Radio 1 breakfast show in order to pass the time during my treatment. A lofty ambition? Perhaps, but I can't say I rate the competition too highly.

Arriving at the hospital so early (8am) conveys a certain sense of urgency, but I doubt anyone even acknowledged my entrance. After showering and moving stuff around in my room, I notice that nothing is happening soon. There are no crashing doors and cries of 'BP 120 over 70, Chem 7 now'. The ward is more B&B than ER.

For the first time I notice my hair, and am struck by a certain sadness at

---

15 Increased appetite is a side effect of steroids.

its imminent loss. I've had a shaved head for the majority of the last two years but I'd just grown my hair. It's the loss of choice and control that I resent. Never mind, at least the chemotherapy should put paid to any risk of (God forbid) growing hair across my back.

Enough of cosmetics, I'm here for a reason and at around 2pm I start my second week of chemo. Much the same as before, I get some funny looking shit pumped into me which makes me kind of tired. This is fine as I catch up on the sleep missed from last night. The uniformed types warn me that the chemo may make my piss develop a hue not unlike Earl Grey tea. I laugh this off, but when the time comes to go the indeed the Earl marches out! I nearly took a photo.

I'm real hungry all day, and I'm finishing my fifth packet of crisps as I write this. I had two lunches and a forbidden piece of cake in the afternoon as well. One mar on my otherwise enjoyable day was the serving of the evening meal. I can appreciate that mistakes happen, but I don't feel that demanding a vegetarian meal is being picky. OK so, my menu choice got mixed up, I said I'd get myself something from the visitor's restaurant to save them the hassle. I don't feel this warranted abuse (well derision at least) from the one member of the staff. Luckily the other nurses were cool, and an alternative was provided. The problem with being in hospital is that you are aware that you are here because you are ill. These people are saving your life every day, and they don't earn nearly enough for it. Therefore complaining seems sacrilegious at least to me, and it especially fucks me off listening to all the whinging old bastards on the ward. However eating a meat meal after 4 years of vegetarianism is not only a complete betrayal of my ethics, but also I would hazard, a serious health risk to my weakened immune system. Whatever, an awkward situation, but one that could not be avoided I guess.

I'm kidding myself about this being a column, it's a fucking diary, isn't it?

WEDNESDAY 30TH SEPTEMBER 1998
Okay, so I'm breaking my rules about writing each day, but I've decided not to try and force anything. I'll briefly re-cap yesterday's events and then carry on from here. Fine.

So yesterday I was allowed to go out into town! For the duration of my stay thus far, my geographical location has been somewhat of an irrelevance as I rarely leave the confines of my chamber. Even when I do I'm transported by car or ambulance as rapidly from this place as possible, so today was an adventure of sorts in what is to become my surrogate home. And Jesus Christ is Boston crap...

I was granted two hours leave to purchase a birthday present for Adi, a period of time I thought woefully inadequate, but oh no, not at all. There is one second hand vinyl store in Boston, which looked promising, but I had little time to peruse. The only other music outlet is the local WH Smiths. There was little else of interest. So I had lunch, bought a CD for my friend and some other knickknacks, and returned to base.

In the evening my Dad came over, and we had a technology night. This involved upgrading this PC to Win 95, installing a modem and CD-ROM, and sorting out my internet account. The nursing staff were rather amused by all the wires and flashing lights that were resplendent about my cubicle, but then commented that I use too much electricity and will tie the phones up downloading porn all night. They're just jealous because I have the most advanced technology on the ward. Unfortunately this gives me a tech overdose, and I don't write anything. I just relax and watch *Airplane*. It is less funny than I remember, and this is disappointing.

So today I wake up eager to check my first batch of email in my new home. Conscious that rumours will no doubt have spread during the night of the Dr Frankenstein patient in room 17 with all the computers and the flashing lights, I am careful not to arouse the suspicion of the patrolling medics. I get the mail protocol set up, I plug in the modem, activate dial up networking. The tone is good, the number dials... and two white coated sentinels come crashing henceforth through my door.

Luckily one of them is my friend Antonio, the other doctor less familiar. I assure them that everything is OK. The strange one begins to say something but Antonio (Dr Pinart, as he is known professionally) reassures him that all is well. Relief. Antonio dismisses the other guardian of public health, and we strike an agreement. He keeps the staff off my back about using phone lines and electricity, I teach him how to use Windows. It seems a fair enough trade. In order to avoid arousing suspicions he examines me quickly as if I were a normal patient, and makes some random inscriptions in his book. A Masonic handshake later and the conspiracy is complete.

So I'm on line again! Oh a return to the world of the living! The joy I had to receive seven fresh mails on my first attempt was indescribable. I'd love to be able to surf around a bit, especially as I installed the latest version of Netscape which seems very impressive, but the risks, my friends, are too great. One must be cautious – these walls have ears.

I felt a little guilty today as my good friend Adi came to visit me on her birthday. It seemed such a shame for her to not be doing anything exciting, especially as the travelling time alone amounted to five hours for the round trip. She seems to enjoy her hastily gathered presents though, so I took some solace. The guys from Leicester also came over and we played yo-yo. We all sucked and myself most of all.

At least I have time on my hands. I have been drawing up little projects to pass the time, and here is what I have so far:

1. Write both this column and other pieces.
2. Read more, especially classics.
3. Improve my yo-yo and juggling skills.
4. Improve my website designing skills, possibly as a source of income if I don't qualify for sickness benefits.
5. Learn conversational Hebrew; I sent off for a free tape so I can talk to Adi in her mother tongue.
6. Make as much use of email as possible and communicate with the masses.
7. And beating leukaemia would be nice.

Numbers

It costs the taxpayer £1100 ($1,700) per week to keep me in a hospital bed. This is before any treatment is administered, just the regular checks and observation. I don't know the exact cost of the medication and chemotherapy, but conservative estimates are double the total cost of keeping me here. I will be here for six months.

My bone marrow transplant will cost the taxpayer approximately £30,000 ($50,000).

I am so glad we have free healthcare here. God bless the NHS. I will never resent paying taxes, I hope.

WEDNESDAY 30TH SEPTEMBER

As if it hasn't been a hectic enough month for us all, Granddad Bill is now very ill, too. We spend our days driving round in a sort of Bermuda

Triangle between Derby, Grantham and Boston. Foolishly, I continue soldiering on at work. Occasionally, the stress proves too much, and weird feelings of guilt surface.

The days are long. After visiting Jonathan, there are numerous phone calls to be made to update relatives and friends. Technical terms need to be repeatedly explained. The other problem is that everyone knows someone who had this or that treatment so why aren't they doing this or that? I state over and over again 'each patient is unique and their treatment is unique to them.' Many misguidedly believe that leukaemia could be 'cut out', removed surgically somehow. They fail to understand what cancer of the blood implies.

Grandma, bless her, offers her words of wisdom: if Jonathan stopped being a vegetarian and ate a good meal of stew or cow pie he would soon be much better.

Everyone talks about bravery, but why don't I have permission to say it's all too much? The not knowing what to say or do, the constant talking to friends and relatives: the travelling, the worrying about how Peter is coping because his father is obviously dying and his son is so ill. And on top of all of this, I'm the one who has to persuade the boys to go and visit Granddad or Jonathan, since 'none of them like hospitals'. Well, who the hell does?

It's a monumental task just to keep going. I calm myself by eating chocolate whilst stroking the cats. I tell them all my troubles, but apparently I've got more than four-cats worth. I keep my inner turmoil very 'inner' and face the world with a smile.

THURSDAY 1ST OCTOBER 1998

A new month and with it new challenges. I wake up today with the yawning chasm of an empty schedule laid bare before me, and it fills me with dread. No chemo, no treatment, no visitors until the evening. I decide that the time has come to read the words that I have been producing for this column these past weeks. I wanted to be realistic about my abilities; I am not a professional columnist nor author. I wanted to remind myself that others may view my work with a slightly less cynical eye than myself, that to theirs it might be fresh, vital and interesting.

Unfortunately, I still found it to be the verbal effluent that I predicted.

Sorry, but I'm not happy with what I have written so far. If you are then I thank you, though I question your judgement. This makes me depressed for some time this afternoon. My major rehabilitation project appears to have been a waste of time. However the sheer volume of empty hours in the day impresses upon me a need to improve and practice, rather than stagnate and relapse into mental impasse. I resolve therefore to improve this dire excuse of a diary, and also to venture beyond this frame and produce more concise stand alone articles.

In other news, I found that David and Thomas are the two most suitable brothers to offer me a bone marrow transplant. Although I would be grateful to either for effectively saving my life, I opt for David as my first choice. He is in better health, is also a vegetarian (less chance of contracting CJD, agree the doctors) and we are closer in both age and relationship. I am still of course indebted to both Thomas and Christopher for volunteering, and my heartfelt thanks are duly extended. Brothers are handy sometimes.

The other good news is that my blood count is good this week, and I can have a whole weekend to play!!! I have a craving for pizza again, as it is never served in hospital. This time I feel like not the sublime delicacies of Pizza Express, but rather the blue-collar charm of Leicester's own Pizza Cottage. Mmmm, jalapenos, green peppers, lots of coleslaw on top. I am still forbidden from eating salad, however, and this saddens me. I am cheered up by a conversation with my friend Tara's Dad. Funny how my situation lubricates conversation with those who I would normally only consider acquaintances. We talk yo-yo's and other such inanities, and I am left in a positive mood about things.

Many of my friends wonder how I maintain my positive outlook, and indeed suggestions have been made that I am in fact in a manic-depressive state. I am happy during the day, because I cry at night. I have to, there is no other choice. Although I don't fear my disease-and I am confident of my health-there is of course an enormous burden on my soul, and catharsis must occur. Crying at night has often been a ritual of mine, it is a natural sedative and frees the mind to sleep, but it is not of course a pleasant experience. But debts must be paid and I pay them most nights but not all. I don't cry about specifics, more about an awareness that my life is running a course over which I have no control. I fear I have reduced this to some surgical diagnosis which is an easy thing to do given my present environment. To put it simply, I'll do my smiling during the day and leave the painful parts until dark.

MONDAY OCTOBER 5TH 1998

Well, the weekend's over and it's back to the office for the 9 to 5. Seriously, it feels like that having to come back to hospital. Just like a job, the day is dull and regimented. I have to report to superiors and supervisors, and I'm expected to behave myself. I don't get paid though. Speaking of money, I just had a great weekend spending some that I don't have. I got my Minidisc which I had so longed for, and a veritable battery of vinyl to copy down onto it. Therapy through commerce, the expenditure of money relieving the gravest of symptoms. I also nearly got into a fight by shouting at some angst-ridden motorist who was harassing an old fellow taking too long to cross the road. It was most exhilarating, but perhaps rather foolish in my condition. I guess I have to express my masculinity some way or another.

But I'm not going to yammer on about shopping or the rest of my rather pleasant weekend. Suffice to say that I'm back in the gulag and this represent the first weekly style instalment of 'My War'. I'm gonna try and keep it more concise from now, but you know how I get carried away...

Two or three interesting happenings for the day, which is quite a catch really. So I just finish watching *Less than Zero* which is better than I thought it would be, and it's time for chemo. There's some drama regarding a block in my Hickmann line, but this soon smoothed out. A ruby sachet[16] is attached to the line and proceeds to fill my vein with its active ingredient. This is the stuff that makes me piss the colour of tea, remember? I'm letting it go about its business, when I notice a red splash on the floor to my side. At first I panic and think that I'm bleeding, but it soon becomes apparent that the damn chemo shit is leaking onto the floor instead of through my veins. The panic button summons an orderly who is swiftly despatched to bring help. A nurse arrives, makes an appraisal of the situation then informs me 'don't worry about the spilt stuff, just stand back, it's dangerous for it to touch your skin.' She shuts the line and leaves to get a replacement valve. It strikes me as odd that it's dangerous for it to touch my skin, but perfectly okay for it to be pumped directly into my veins. Go figure.

Next big bit of news is that the DSS inform me that I am not eligible for invalidity benefits. The reason? I have not paid enough national insurance in the last 2 years. I was in fucking university! What the fuck? You go to college so you can get a good job, you work during the vacations (and pay

---

16 Doxarubucin, a chemotherapy drug used in the treatment of leukaemia.

plenty NI thanks very fucking much) and then when you're sick they tell you to fucking die! Bastards! I'm so furious when I hear this that words simply escape me. I've calmed down a bit now and figure that if I cant get invalidity then I'll just sign on for regular jobseeker's allowance. That'll be a right laugh applying for jobs: Days available for work – none, special skills – leukaemia suffering. I can see finding employment may take some time. If at the end of the day I can't claim any benefits whatsoever, then I take back everything I said about paying taxes last week.

Finally, I just went for a walk in the miserable precipitation lingering beyond the miserable incarceration of my hospital room. As I left, the nurses commented on my freshly shaved head, and curiously my manner of dress. When I told them I was going for a walk they told me that I should watch out for security 'dressed like that'. Apparently wearing a dark coat with a hood, in rainy weather, is what criminals do.

WEDNESDAY 7TH OCTOBER 1998

Hmm, rather tired and disappointed at myself for not writing much recently. Ups and downs over the last two days really. Tuesday afternoon was real depressing. My hospital room seemed smaller than ever as I attempted to fill the dreaded 4pm – 6pm pre dinner slot. Phone calls to all my friends yielded no response, and I couldn't face either my books or my toys. Even my music sounded flat and uninspired. I was atrophying in my hospital bed, and I had a desperate desire for human contact. Fortunately my Mum came to the rescue, and then later on Jay, Tara and Adam. God, I'd go insane without visitors – the nurses are real nice and all, but they'll never be a substitute for friends and family. I just want to hang out like regular people. It doesn't help much that Boston is such a crap journey from everywhere. If my friends take the train from Leicester it's a five hour round trip, so they have to dedicate a whole day to it. On the other hand; I am cheered up by the favourable responses I received to the first instalment of this column. Thanks to everyone who took the time to read it.

Food is becoming a problem. Not a problem like the hospital is introducing rationing or anything, but my diet seems intrinsically linked to the monotonous regime of hospital life. The vegetarian menu is the same every day, every week. It has about 12 choices, of which six are OK, two are edible and the rest contain nuts to which I am allergic. This means that on a two main meal a day diet, I have little variation throughout the week. Another problem is that of the 8 edibles, at least five have cheese as a strong motif. My menu choices get ignored a lot, and I reached breaking point today when I received broccoli and cheese bake. Wouldn't be so bad except that my last four meals were potato, cheese and leek bake; cauliflower cheese; spinach and mushroom lasagne with lots of cheese; and broccoli and cheese bake again. I go to the visitor's canteen for food, but they're obsessed with cheese as well. It also costs like £3.50 for a meal. I swear being in hospital, especially when you're on steroids that make you ravenous, is an expensive business. I need to eat continuously, but my food options are limited. I'm glad I'm not a vegan now – I can't even eat sandwiches or salads, due to risk of infection in uncooked food. And if you don't like cheese well....

On the good side I resumed reading today. If I can't satisfy my appetite for food, I can at least attempt to appease my intellectual cravings. I resumed reading *One Hundred Years of Solitude* half way through, after the onset of my illness caused me to suspend reading it. I read the entire second half in one afternoon. If you have not read this book, read it now. I was quite proud of myself for spending my time reading and not on the Playstation that was so kindly donated to me by Adam last night. Hey, I appreciate the gift though.

SUNDAY 11TH OCTOBER 1998
Yes, I know it's been a while since my last entry, but hey I'm trying to be concise these days. So to catch up on treatment and stuff, I'm now on a course of daily chemotherapy injections. They're OK and all, but it means coming in everyday, even on weekends for the jab. Never mind, at least I got out for a while.

This week has been thought provoking as regards my illness. You see no matter how many injections and IV drips I have, I still find it hard to convince myself that there's actually anything wrong with me. I suffer no physical ill effects of the treatments, and visitors comment on how well I look, not how sickly. So when Dr Barrowby (undoubtedly spelt wrong) warns against any kind of human contact the weekend, it's real hard to take him seriously. Still, one has to be responsible and I obey most of the rules they set me (I still eat untoasted bread, AND I had a sip of beer!).

Of course the other major factor of my hospital tenure is the relentless monotony, about which I monotonously moan. I had to face some home truths this week. For this I thank both the consultant Dr Tringham, and my friend Adi. I have to face up to the fact that I am going to be here for 6 months, and I'm only three weeks into it. I just have to deal with it. I needed the impetus of others to bring me to this realisation. I can't expect to just be granted compassionate leave whenever I get a little bored. I'm quite proud of myself for coming to this revelation, and I'm actually looking forward to the coming week. I guess the best way to look at the start of the new week is that it's one week closer to the end of my treatment, rather than the beginning of another 5 day stretch. As part of this new mindset I hope to make better use of my time, particularly as regards reading and writing. I know that I can't begin another week like last week: terminal depression by Tuesday afternoon is not going to aid my recovery.

One piece of crap news – Midland Bank were very kind the other week, promising a compassionate treatment of my account due to my most unfortunate medical condition. They began their compassionate treatment this week by revoking my credit card. Thanks.

But to round off this week, I'm happy to say that my room has been upgraded in my absence and I now have my own fridge! Cool! Any visitors are now more than welcome to bring offerings of Diet Coke and Marks and Spencer's ready-made meals. I also finally have a place to put the fridge magnet that Naomi sent me. Tomorrow I have some chemo that I've kinda been dreading: a lumbar tap. It involves a hole in my lower back and some sort of suction affair. Afterwards I have lie on my back for 6 hours without rising. Can't be much fun, but I got a whole stack of movies in, fIREHOSE on Minidisc and a fridge full of fine food, so it can't be too bad I guess...

MONDAY 12TH OCTOBER 1998

At 8am my pager starts beeping, and I know then that my Grandfather is dead. The message says 'call Dad', but it's a formality. He passed away at 1.30am, peacefully and dignified. I think we're all glad it's over, and that he's at peace. My dad is going to spend the day with Grandma, whilst I reflect on things from my room. I haven't really got much more to say about it.

So big chemo today. I have the ruby red 'makes your piss look like tea' stuff, the injection in the arm and of course the lumbar puncture awaits in the afternoon. I have to give a massive blood sample from my left arm, which is quite painful afterwards, but the results show an unexpected rise in my platelet count, which is good. The lumbar puncture itself is a bit of anti-climax. I'm bracing myself for drills and bonesaws, but not even the anaesthetic injection is of any great consequence. Within ten minutes I have a huge plaster across my lumbar region, and I'm on my back for six hours. It wasn't as difficult as I thought it would be, but I still managed to soak myself with piss (the colour of tea, of course) whilst attempting to urinate into a cardboard bottle. This is annoying, but I can't do much about it as I have to stay on my back. I ride it out.

If last week was a revelation for accepting my hospital internment, today was a bit of a wake up call for accepting that I am ill. The sheer quantity of medical treatment today kind of enforced the fact that I do have a serious disease and that I am at risk of being in a lot worse condition than at present.

I am not surprised to find out that I will not be able to attend my Granddad's funeral, and I resign myself to not being able to attend Halloween parties and the like. Never mind, one has to be realistic about these things. It's still odd to say to yourself 'you have leukaemia, you have cancer'. I wouldn't say that admitting this plunged me into depression; it was more like a slap round the face. To reiterate my attitude towards boredom: just deal with it. The nurse has just mentioned to me that I'm borderline anaemic, and I will probably have a blood transfusion in the next couple of days[17]. I told you I was ill.

WEDNESDAY 14TH OCTOBER 1998
It's one of those moments when every phone dial returns either an engaged tone or no answer, and you're looking at the clock thinking 'does this mean they're on the way to visit me, or have they just gone out?' Five emails in the inbox, but three are trash, the other two pleasant but short. No one has called all day. Still I'm not resentful (honest!), it's just it always seems to work out that my parents and friends all visit on the day that the phone doesn't stop ringing, and then you get days like this when you don't say more than 'two sugars and milk please' all day.

Some excitement though – we just had a power cut! It only lasted for like a second, but as you can imagine this can have serious consequences in a hospital. Things started beeping, the alarm went off, everyone's 'call a nurse' light came on, all sorts of shit. The staff ran around for five minutes doing things, and then they were nowhere to be found for the next half an hour which was weird. Maybe they were all collecting batteries and candles or something. Things appear to have returned to normal now, but I'm glad I'm not on life support at the moment. Probably going to

---

17 Anaemia means the body's haemoglobin is low, and the patient will require a blood transfusion.

have a blood transfusion tomorrow so they'd better have it sorted by then.

Went into town today and bought the *Easy Rider* soundtrack from a second hand record store. I asked the guy at the counter if he had *Kick out the Jams* by the MC5. I told him it was recorded in 1969, Elektra records, etc. He insisted it would probably be in the '70's / 80's Pop Groups' section if he had it. Strangely, it did not appear next to the Culture Club, Thompson Twins and Bay City Rollers vinyl. Still my one purchase looks promising; it's just a shame I won't be near a record player for the next two weeks.

I'm getting more accustomed to this feeling ill business. I have to wash myself with 'hibiscrub'[18] now, a rather caustic, but strangely refreshing lotion. Worryingly the bottle comes with the warning 'avoid contact with the brain.' This I do. My right arm is all fucked up – apparently I've pulled the ligaments somehow and a bruise has appeared on my forearm. I'm developing sores and dry skin across the back of my neck and shoulders – this apparently heralds imminent hair loss. I was also totally exhausted walking into town today (a rare treat), and I had to eat as soon as I got there. Then I had to resign myself to taking a taxi back. Not good. Oh and my blood sugar level is very high today, and I look even more anaemic and urgh... Am I getting carried away here?

My new plaything for killing dead time is planning for my holiday which I WILL be taking shortly after my 21st birthday and recovery from leukaemia. It will be the completion of my visits to America before I move on to explore the rest of the world. So far the plan is this:

After working for three months or so I will fly to New York City in mid-August. I'll spend a week or two in my favourite city then travel westward towards California. I don't have time to do the whole country, so a couple of stops for like four or five days at time. Chicago is appealing, as is a more southern route, though maybe too hot at that time of year. Whatever, I'll figure it out while I'm there. Then hook up with the kutha crew[19] in North California, explore around bit, maybe see LA, or even Mexico, then fly back to NYC for a few days and then home. Total of around six weeks I reckon, just in time to go back to Uni.

---

18 A strong disinfectant to clean the body; many hospitals do not advocate the use of this lotion for regular use of patients with leukaemia.
19 The kutha crew are the nickname for Mike Woodburn's gang of friends.

Better start saving those dole cheques.

THURSDAY 15TH OCTOBER 1998
Shit.

Something not good has happened. I'm in the kitchen making myself a Cupasoup, and on the off chance my day to day doctor, an Armenian who goes by the name of Denton pops in. He asks how I am, and then as if he's discussing the weather just drops a total fucking bombshell. My brothers are not a suitable match for the bone marrow transplant. The rogue cells, which is what they were testing, will in fact render them incompatible. He casually mentions that we now have to find an unrelated donor. I am of course caught a bit off guard about this and his rather casual attitude. Only 2 weeks ago he was saying how good it was that my brothers matched, as finding a non related donor is very difficult. Now he's all 'well, there's billions of people in this world.' My head aches, and for the first time, I think I'm scared.

OK, I have had a few hours to take in these latest revelations. Oh shit, they're coming to give me some blood now, and it's going to get tricky with my computer all plugged in. I'll leave this till tomorrow. No, there's no time like the present. I'm hooked up to a new supply of blood now, and I particularly want to avoid staring at the viscous red fluid globulating through plastic pipes into my body. I'm having a 'what am I doing here?' moment, so I think I'll take my mind of things by writing some more.

My head hurts. I've asked for paracetomol like three times now, and it's beginning to annoy me.

Good news, though, is that I can go home again this weekend as I am apparently making a very good recovery. This came as a result of a conversation I had with my consultant this afternoon regarding the whole transplant fuck up. More of that later, but she bore the rather unexpected news that I may be in full remission! Can you believe it? They're going to do a bone marrow test next week, which they predict will confirm that I am, for the time being, leukaemia free. This does not mean I am cured (though there is a slight chance), but rather for now I would be a healthy human being. The thing is that the cancer can and most probably will return at any time, but being in remission is most definitely good news. It means my treatment is working, I can have a week off chemotherapy and the transplant should be easier. Speaking of which they now have to look (again this word, probably) for a non-related donor. They aren't very good with terminology here. I was informed that the 'panel of donors' would be searched for a match. Now to me a panel is a body consisted of five or six experts in a particular field, this would undoubtedly prove a very small selection of people for possible transplant. The 'panel' as it turns out refers to a database of over 1 million UK donors and 25 million world-wide[20]. I would call this a register or perhaps even a catalogue. Panel just sounds scarily small. Anyway they seem confident enough of finding a match, and are rather proud to tell me that recent transplants have come from as far afield as Vancouver and Frankfurt. Better clear out any dormant xenophobia if there's gonna be a risk of an international donation.

FRIDAY 16TH OCTOBER 1998

God, if there's one thing I hate it's being patronised. Barrowby and the gang come round to check on how I'm doing and all that. Everything is OK and he confirms that I can be released for the weekend. This is good, and while he's here I ask for some further clarification on the situation with my brothers. Now, OK I don't expect him to describe it all in technical terms, but I expect something a little more medical than 'well you have a string of pebbles, and your Brother has a string of pebbles, and if the colours don't match, well then you can't make the jigsaw and it doesn't work.' The fucker, what does he take me for? Besides I wasn't even asking about that... I can't be bothered to press the point with him, and I decide to wait to see Dr Tringham who is far more helpful in such matters. I don't want to start resenting those who are working to save my life and cure my disease, but Denton and Barrowby are definitely in my bad books at the moment, whilst Tringham and Antonio are definite stars. The two Iraqi doctors don't speak much.

An awkward situation arose earlier. I was minding my own business, playing Tetris when I heard knock at my door. I presumed it to be one of the nurses come to take my temperature, and was therefore caught rather off guard when a rather tall man of the cloth poked his head inside. He informed me that he was 'doing the rounds' and wondered if I would like a chat. Now normally I'd be happy for any company, but as I am of no religious persuasion, I was hesitant to invite in a vicar. This made me feel uncomfortable, and I gave a flat 'no'. It seemed rather rude of me, but I

---

20 In the UK, this database of donors (to which as many people as possible are encouraged to sign up) is maintained by the Anthony Nolan Trust, details of which may be found at the end of this book.

guess he understood. He departed with a 'looks like you're keeping your-self busy anyway,' which was odd as I was just wasting time on my Gameboy. It is good of such people to give up their time to help others, but I couldn't dispel images of condemned men giving confession before going to the electric chair. An odd situation.

Another odd situation was that the other night we were warned to be on the lookout for a 'prowler' who had been seen round the hospital, prowl-ing presumably. We had to close our windows and everything. Most exciting.

I'm going to sign off this week's entry now so that I can make the most of my weekend. Fingers crossed for that bone marrow test on Monday.

MONDAY 19TH OCTOBER 1998

The Day of Reckoning. Dr Hamid is very jovial when he pops in to per-form my bone marrow test. His optimism is encouraging, and I have no qualms as he goes about preparing sharp metal objects to plunge through my sternum. Luckily he also provides anaesthetic, so it's not as traumatic as one might fear. It is quite unusual to have a 4 inch long inkwell screwed into the centre of your chest though. To this a syringe is attached and a most unusual sensation occurs as the bone marrow is sucked out of the cartilage. Dr Hamid is very excited as he collects the sample. The small white deposits are, he ensures me, a sign that I am well on the way to com-plete remission, and he hurries them off to the labs for further testing. This good news is further strengthened by his assurance that I can leave the hospital as soon as my medicine is ready, about 12.30pm.

So at 4.00pm I've had the car loaded up for three hours (I have to take all my shit with me) and the medicine still hasn't arrived. I'm a bit annoyed as I could have made my Granddad's funeral if it had arrived when it should have. It finally turns up in time for me to hit the rush hour traffic back at Grantham and miss any chance of sorting out my benefits strife today.

I unload all my gear and I wait for the family to return from the funeral. Mum and brothers arrive first, Dad sometime later. It transpires that I was main topic of conversation, and this makes me feel a little uneasy. Even a prayer was dedicated to me and my plight. I'm sure it was all well meant, but I feel as if I hijacked the occasion in my own absence. The local paper printed a glowing tribute to my Grandfather and asked for donations to be sent to Leukaemia charities. Apparently everyone was asking about me, which is nice and all, but my brothers commented that many of them didn't even know who I was and thought they were the ones with leukaemia. Another of those odd situations that seem to arise when you have a serious disease – well meant gestures, often from strangers, that make for uncomfortable exchanges. In a way I'm glad I wasn't there, if it meant becoming the centre of attention at my own Granddad's funeral.

MONDAY 19TH OCTOBER

Off to Granddad's funeral today. Jonathan is totally frustrated by the fact he's not allowed to attend. I rush out of work at twelve o'clock. I could have taken the whole day off, but by working that morning I have saved the school budget £60 in supply cover costs. Granddad, an ex headmaster, would have approved.

Truth is, it was really a ploy, an excuse, because I couldn't face sitting at Grandma's (my mother-in-law) all morning, and if I couldn't face it why should the boys? We arrive just in time to set off to the Crematorium. On arrival I park the car, and at last I don't have to pay! I had the change ready just in case.

We all assemble in a foyer: Peter constantly asks me who everyone is. Why do men expect you to remember all of their relatives and friends of the family for them? There are one or two people who I do not recognise. I ask my sister in law, but she doesn't know either. Do some people just attend funerals as a means of passing the time? Is it a hobby? Like trainspotting?

We venture into the inner sanctum; it's just like being in church. The boys look distinctly uncomfortable. As a family we don't 'do' religion. Things get worse when the vicar enters. I don't think the vicar would have recognised Granddad if they passed in the street, but he's here presiding over the proceedings. The hymns cause a problem for such a non-religious bunch: even with the service sheets we were all a little out of time and tune.

The vicar talked about Granddad. It was very interesting until he began to express Granddad's (or were they really his own?) opinions regarding the present state of the teaching profession. As most of the family and friends were teachers this was not the most opportune moment to tackle such a controversial subject.

Then it was time to pray. I assumed it would be for Granddad, but we also ended up saying a few prayers for Jonathan. An announcement is made: the proceeds from the collection and donations in lieu of flowers will go to

Leukaemia Research.

We return to Grandma's. The best family bone china tea service is out, and the table laden with magnificent WI tea: I help serve it. Whilst taking a plate of cakes round a family friend enquires, 'Who the hell is Jonathan?' Needless to say, I am glad to return home. On Grandma's insistence we have brought Granddad's wreath back with us. No, I don't know why either. I set it on the dining table, because what do you do with a funeral wreath?. The next morning I find one of the cats fast asleep in the middle of it.

Frankly, it's been a hell of a week all round. The bombshell about Thomas and David both proving to be unsuitable donors has dropped. I can't believe it. Surely we didn't all get it wrong. Did we? They did tell us it would be easy didn't they- three brothers- fantastic odds. Why give out false hope? Why be so certain before an event? Ok, you say, we must have misunderstood. No, wrong, not all six of us! Why didn't the doctors use phrases like perhaps *or* likely *or* wait and see.

But, as usual, there's no time to dwell on this. Jonathan needs even more patience, love, understanding and food. Dr B really put his foot in it by not recognising Jonathan's high level of intelligence. At least he didn't make the ultimate faux pas of all by telling Peter and myself and not Jonathan. Jonathan is 20 years old, an adult patient in his own right. Just because Mum and Dad are around does not mean all questions and comments should be addressed to them – those that are guilty of this please note.

And me? My feelings of fear, anger, love are all put on hold. Let's just take it a day at a time. Of course, there's no other choice.

THURSDAY 22ND OCTOBER 1998

Oh, so I haven't written anything in a while. I've been so tired you see. I guess you could say I've actually been feeling ill. I think I probably tired myself out on Tuesday by going to Leicester to visit university and then Lincoln in the evening. University was a bit of a let down. Most people couldn't even be bothered to say hello, but that's their problem I guess. Some people just don't know what to do in these situations, but then again we were never the most tight knit group on campus. I checked out the pictures of the academic year I'll be joining next September. For some reason they don't look as nice as my original year. Maybe it's just me.

My benefit saga drags on... The visit to the dole office was most dispiriting. I realise now that my medical condition is not going to elicit much sympathy from those on the other side of the desk. They've heard it all before and probably from as many bogus as genuine applicants. They were particularly unimpressed that I should ask for my claim to be back paid, even though it was on their recommendation that I spent a month pursuing incapacity benefit. Oh, whatever, I guess it's slowly getting sorted.

A marked contrast was made when I met with the Macmillan Nurse at Grantham Hospital. For those of you not familiar with the Macmillan Trust, it's a charity that provides assistance to people living with cancer. The nurse was totally cool and promised to help out with the swine at the benefit agency. She also put in a claim for me to get a grant from the trust to help pay for stuff. I agreed to this on the basis that I would repay it when I start earning money again. Anyway, more than the security of money, it's nice to know that there are some people who are sympathetic to your situation and genuinely want to help out. It was a refreshing change after a stressful morning with unsmiling officials.

Other good news though – my bone marrow results! Yes, I made it into complete remission; that is to say less than 1% of my cells are cancerous. This is pretty cool considering I was at 98% at one stage. My blood counts were also good, so they predicted that I could go ahead with Stage 2 on Monday. The other option was to give me another week off to recover my white blood cells a bit, but yet again I'm responding too well and forcing myself back into treatment. I guess the sooner I start the sooner I finish though. Anyway Dr Tringham informs me that I'll get to enjoy another lumbar puncture on Monday, so that's something to look forward to.

I just looked at myself in the mirror, and I barely recognised myself. My face seems pale but puffed out. My ribs are showing, but my stomach is bloated. I'm very tired and it's only 11am. I'm quite proud of myself for writing today's entry, because I'm in a lethargic mood today. I have all this time on my hands, and I just can't seem to do anything with it. I either can't be bothered to do anything constructive, or I'm just too tired to act upon my motivations. As I mentioned at the beginning of today's entry, I am feeling the effects of my illness (or is it the treatment?) now and it's frustrating. I really just want to get on with normal life – something that I became acutely aware of when I went to university the other day. Having leukaemia is, for want of a better word, an inconvenience, a rather large inconvenience. I wish I had some company during the day.

I forget sometimes that my friends have jobs and study to attend to. It's annoying that I'm usually more motivated to write and be constructive in the evenings. It's filling these empty mornings and afternoons that's the problem. Well, I'm a bit tired now, I think I need a rest.

SUNDAY 25TH OCTOBER 1998

I appear to have regained some of that lost energy, which is problematic to a certain extent as it requires me to find something to occupy myself with. I had a bit of a career and life crisis the other day, but reading this morning's *Observer* motivates me towards writing again. Ironically I appear to have little to put in today's diary. Instead I resolve once more to write some other articles, this time I actually come up with a few ideas and promise myself to begin them this week. I also finally get round to helping my Dad with building a website for the company he works for. It isn't as painful as I thought it might be, and certainly will be less so than tomorrow's lumbar tap. Yes, the great thing about making good progress with my blood counts is that I get to enjoy the more uncomfortable treatments sooner. Tomorrow sees the beginning of the much hyped 'Phase 2' of my treatment. One can only wonder as to what delights lie beyond...

MONDAY 26TH OCTOBER 1998

I've just spent six hours lying on my back, which is not exactly my idea of a fun afternoon. On the plus side I mastered the art of pissing prostrate and avoided any kind of urinal spillage. On the down side I was in a foul mood to begin with and even this little victory could do little to change that. I woke up this morning feeling crap with the aching in my legs having spread to my arms. This aside I am frustratingly contemplative this morning, with that old chestnut 'why me?' driving me to distraction. It strikes me today that I am missing out on a year in the 'prime of my life'. Previously my age had not been an issue. I had just seen my treatment as a temporary obstacle to my current plans, plans that will continue uninterrupted as soon as the obstacle is overcome. Today it strikes me that 20 is a particularly unfortunate age to have to endure this inconvenience. Though there is never a good age to develop such a malady, I will be spending my 20th year living the life of a 70 year old. I purchase a copy of *The Face* today and am reminded that for the next six months at least I will not be clubbing, meeting new people, going to gigs, behaving irresponsibly – in short living as any other person my age would be.

I spend the afternoon in my new but not improved hospital room trying to overcome this self pity. Fortunately as much as *The Face* reminds me what I am missing, it also reminds me of what I have to look forward to and how much I will appreciate it when I'm healthy.

As Dr Hamid applies the lumbar tap I resign myself to another six hours staring at the ceiling. Fortunately, a surprise visit from my brother David and his girlfriend Jo help pass the time. I watch a movie and read some and I'm feeling OK, but this nagging self pity is still dogging me from earlier in the day. It takes a great deal of effort to write, but I feel that if I attempt to express myself in writing then I may resolve some of the issues that would otherwise keep me awake all night.

I sometimes feel like I've achieved absolutely nothing in my admittedly short life: I have no girlfriend and have never managed to form any kind of serious relationship, I'm not doing as well as I should at university, I'm grossly in debt – not that any of these things should matter, but they do when you've got all day with nothing to do but think about them. In normal situations like this a well meaning sort will usually comment 'well at least you've got your health.' Oh, well.

WEDNESDAY 28TH OCTOBER 1998
Don't worry, I've cheered myself up. Monday's entry was hopelessly defeatist, I know. Still I have to exorcise these demons occasionally, and it just so happens that this is my medium.

Yesterday I had my visit from the consultants, but this time they had brought some bright young things with them. In addition to the five doctors and one nurse there were two or three fresh faced medical students in tow. This made for a lot of white coats in one room, which was rather intimidating. I was reminded of Richard Burton's spoken introduction to the *War of the Worlds* musical 'as scientists study bacteria that swarm and multiply in a drop of water.'

Barrowby rather annoyingly ignored me and addressed me via the students. Example: 'so you see he will be having chemotherapy for the rest of the week and we may let him out for the weekend.' Tringham was her usual congenial self however, and I almost got the feeling that she was trying to set me up with one of the med students, commenting on how we were both vegetarians and we both study at Leicester University. Probably my imagination though.

Good news! Finally got my money from the DSS, including back payments! I take back all the nasty things I said about them.

On a down note I develop some kind of sickness this afternoon. It seemed to pass, but it completely ruined my 'do something constructive' initiative which I had planned to start this afternoon. I watched the Booker prize awards[21] the other night and decided that I would quite like to win it someday. This may be a little ambitious, especially as I have never written any fiction, but it's a good a target as any.

It is frustrating that I have so much time on my hands but make relatively little use of it. The environment is admittedly uninspiring, but I feel I'm guilty of making excuses. I have so many things I've promised myself to do, but I usually find something else to interrupt the planned course of events. The one activity I pursue with any commitment is reading, which I figure is research rather than diversion from my writing, so I guess it serves a dual purpose. As the school teacher said: 'must try harder.'

MONDAY NOVEMBER 2ND 1998

OK, so I don't write anything at all when I'm out of hospital, but I've got better things to do, OK? Great weekend with a suitably ghoulish Halloween courtesy of Tony and Celene. The horror has impinged upon my weekday existence though – I awoke this morning to find hair all over the pillow. Yes, I am losing my hair. Goddamn, this is supposed to happen at 55, not 20. I took the bull by the horns though and borrowed the hospitals clippers and shaved it close, real close. It was a bit scary though, because as I shaved I pulled more hair out, and I swear halfway through I was nearly crying. I looked, for want of a better word, shit. The finished result isn't too bad, just desperately thin in places. In a couple of weeks I'm going to be billiard ball smooth. Time to invest in a new hat I think.

Plans for the day: blood transfusion, lumbar puncture, spend six hours on my back. Looks like I'll have plenty of time to read then. As a little treat, I was brought pizza for lunch today. I get the feeling that there must be something very bad due to happen, as it was the nicest meal I have ever had here.

THURSDAY 5TH NOVEMBER 1998

Remember, remember, the 5th of November... I doubt I'll be remembering this one for any particular reason, very nondescript indeed. I haven't written too much (anything!) over the last few days because I've been a little bit ill and a little bit busy. The illness has included real back-to-basics throw-up-your-lunch stuff on Tuesday. The best part was that I

---

21 *Amsterdam* by Ian MacEwan won the Booker Prize in 1998.

was on the phone to my friend Naomi whilst I was being sick – she got the full audio version! I've also had the worst headaches, a side effect of Monday's lumbar puncture. The headaches are a frustrating thing, not for the actual discomfort caused, but for the disruption that entails. I have all this free time to do constructive things, and as you know, I've been cursing my lack of motivation. So when I finally get around to writing or whatever else it is I want to do, it's real annoying to have a headache come along and fuck my plans up. Could be worse, I suppose. At least I haven't had any horrid infections like the other leukaemia patients.

I got my own back on that patronising bastard Barrowby (I checked the spelling). He asked how I was, 'fine apart from the headaches'. He asked whereabouts. I responded, 'In my head'. He didn't get the joke. The pretty young med-student laughed though...

My hair has stopped falling out for the moment. I started wearing a hat around hospital, but people stared at me even more than with my super-short hair. I quite like the idea of hats though, and I think I might start collecting them. I already have about five or six, and I think a huge collection would be quite a cool thing. I'm such a glutton for ownership! I love the idea of owning things. *Damn* I'm such a consumer. I don't need lots of hats, but I want them anyway. I don't need to own books, but I would rather buy them than borrow them at the moment. Terrible really. I'm not surprised my finances are in such bad shape.

Oooh, I feel another headache coming on...

SATURDAY 7TH NOVEMBER 1998

The headaches have been getting worse. You catch me now in a brief respite from the barrage of abuse that my brain is enduring at present. The lack of fluid in my meninges is causing my cerebrum to buffet the interior of my cranium ,and this causes immense discomfort. In layman's terms – my head hurts when I move. Consequently I have spent much of the past 48 hours lying on my back and this accounts for the lack of diary entries. In fact, the journey home was so unpleasant I decorated the hard shoulder of the A52 with my lunch. Anyway, it is, as it were, the calm before the storm, so I'll drop anchor and fill you in on the news.

The news being not altogether good, mind. So Dr Tringham comes in to see me, and thankfully she hasn't brought Barrowby with her this time. The Iraqi doctors have recruited a new member and there are now three of them. The new guy seems nice enough, but things get confusing when

I realise that all three of them are called Mohammed. This is complicated by the fact that everyone likes to be on first name terms, and I can't read the surnames on their badges. I know the chubby one is called Hamid, but the other two seem destined to remain Mohammed and Mohammed. This reminds me of Thompson and Thompson in Herge's Adventures of Tin Tin for some reason.

Anyway.... Dr Tringham informs me that there are two potential donors for me in the shape of two men in their mid-fifties. This is a good thing, but Dr Tringham is hesitant. When pressed she informs me that my marrow type is extremely rare and final tests will need to be done top prove their suitability. She also warns that I may be too rare to ever receive a transplant. If this is the case then I will require a two year treatment program as an out patient. My response to this is a complete and utter unwillingness to accept facts, and I pretend she hasn't said it.

Later, I digest it more responsibly, but I'm still insistent on receiving a transplant. Someone has stolen my life and I want it back! In slightly better news, Dr Tringham informs me that phase 3 of my treatment will be carried out in Nottingham Hospital. This is good as Nottingham is an infinitely better place than Boston, and it makes travelling much easier for friends and family. On the down side, phase 3 will begin on December 6th. Therefore it will finish on December 27th. No breaks are allowed. It is the most intense part of my treatment. I'd better get some good presents this year...

WEDNESDAY 18TH NOVEMBER 1998

Not in the best mood today. Yesterday the doctors arrived en masse, about seven or eight at least, clad head to foot in quarantine gear. It appears that I am now so susceptible to infection that anyone entering my room should don a mask and apron. This created the impression of being attended to by an army of robots, particularly as I have developed an odd echoing sound in my hearing which gives people's voices an oddly mechanical tone. Obviously I am aware that these procedures are for my benefit, but it does convey a kind of bubonic plague atmosphere. It seemed particularly odd for my parents to have to wear masks, but for the best I guess...

I sleep a lot at the moment which is both a blessing and a curse. On the one hand it passes the time and staves off the loneliness that characterises my day. Conversely napping during the day makes me even more tired and dependent upon further sleep. I also have disturbing dreams. Perhaps it's the hospital ambient sound impinging upon my slumber, but I usually dream about unpleasant medical scenarios. Today I dreamt that my treatment had resulted in a complete loss of my locomotive skills. I crashed to the floor whilst walking across the room, my head impacting upon a sharp corner causing severe injury. There was blood all over my hands, and I woke up with my right arm paralysed by pins and needles. Not spooky or anything, just unpleasant.

Sleeping in the day is also unpleasant, but sleeping at night is worse. I feel an acute sense of isolation and loneliness at night, especially as I'm sleeping in a building full of strangers. It sounds like a bad chat up line, but just once it would be nice to have some company, to not have to wake up alone.

FRIDAY NOVEMBER 20TH 1998

Hey, feeling a bit more positive today. Derek, my travelling friend came over from Amsterdam en route to Zurich. His wacky Californian ways proved a hit with the medical staff and cheered me up a treat. I even managed to ignore the mask after a while. A nurse admitted today that the aprons served a 'mainly psychological purpose.' What exactly does that mean? So anyway big ups to Derek, and also Harriet for the natty mobile she constructed for me. Happy Birthday to my friend Jay. Gutted that I can't make the party, but I guess there'll be others. Thanks to everyone who called or visited in this rather difficult week.

Friday night inside. Unfortunately Children in Need dominates tonight's television schedules. A noble cause, but terrible programming. Luckily a steady stream of American sitcoms is provided by channels 2 and 4. I'm really itching to go back to the US after seeing Derek again. Sitcoms will have to do for the time being. Hopefully I'll be on the outside next weekend though, even it if I only go as far as Grantham or Lincoln. We'll see.

SATURDAY 21ST NOVEMBER 1998

A melancholy day breeds a melancholy mood. Dr Tringham didn't sound positive about donors. I get the feeling that searching for a match is quite tiresome, and NHS doctors are overworked as hell. Antonio was pulling another 18 hour shift, for the 100th day in a row or something and he had flu.. I told him to go home (as much for my safety as his), but he wouldn't. Tringham dissed him; in her day they did 165 hours a week don't you know? So he stood on the other side of the glass and watched. I have a rash on my feet, sores in my mouth and blood in my toilet bowl. This is considered progress, and good progress at that.

SUNDAY 22ND NOVEMBER 1998

As I've mentioned before, I don't enjoy nights in hospital much. When the lights go out, there is a period of silence as the inhabitants, sedated and exhausted drift off to sleep. I'm usually awake at this time, writing my diary, or reading perhaps. As I prepare myself for sleep the painkillers wear off, and as I close my eyes, the moaning and screaming starts. It's not very nice, but it allows me to cry unnoticed.

TUESDAY 24TH NOVEMBER 1998

I'm so very tired. I probably sleep two-thirds of the day, and spend the rest sat up in bed. My mouth ulcers have swollen into bilious blisters which make swallowing the disgusting hospital food even more difficult. I had a conversation with Antonio about European cuisine. I don't know how he can cope with English food after having spent most of his life in Spain. I would have moved to Italy so I could at least get a decent meal.

On a more serious note, the doctors appear to be resigning themselves to not being able to find me a bone marrow transplant. For some reason their claims that they have never failed to find a donor for a patient have now been readjusted to '95% of patients don't find donors'. I'm not sure what to think and for a while I'm extremely depressed. I am now attempting to come to terms with another 2 years of treatment, albeit as an out-patient, if a donor cannot be found. I'm trying not to think about it too much.

THURSDAY 26TH NOVEMBER

Maybe the nocturnal anguishes of my fellow internees is intruding upon my sleep, but I have been having peculiarly vivid dreams of late. Last I night I first dreamt that I was test driving a rather battered Porsche 924, a seventies model. I was completely unprepared for its performance and had great difficulty controlling the car as I raced around at high speeds. Upon an imminent collision I stamped on the brake, and as I did so my foot lashed out and kicked the bottom of the bed. I woke up with the clock reading 5.10am and a bruised big toe. I then returned to sleep and embarked upon another memorable excursion into never never land. I was in my parents' house changing a lightbulb on the landing. A workman came in and offered to help. I told him I had the job taken care of, so he offered to fix the rest of the place up. I heard him leave some time later and went to see what he had altered. From the lounge window I could see that the garden had been flooded to the level of the patio with turquoise coloured water. Floating on the water was an armada of origami swans made of white paper, and large green tissues that resembled water lilies.

I was overcome by the beauty of the scene. I therefore felt the urge to share it with someone and raced off in my car to find a female friend. When I found her and brought her back the water had drained from the garden and the paper swans were hanging from the washing line, drying out in the sun. I found this most distressing.

Well any amateur Freudian (or is it Jungian?) scholars can draw the appropriate Oedipus Complex conclusions from this if they so desire. Returning to the world of the living, well, not a lot to say really. The doctors reassured my anxious Father (and myself) that they are indeed doing everything they can to find a donor. My mouth is still sore and the light bulb in the shower has still not been fixed from two days ago. I imagine the trauma of urinating in the dark was the basis of my second dream. Hopefully I'll be going home tomorrow, even though the nurses are still wearing masks when entering my room.

The wisdom of Doctor Denton:
    'Don't think too much for it strains the brain.'
    'Just wait, and God will open a door.'

SUNDAY 29TH NOVEMBER 1998
Well the last few days have been a bit of a mixed bag. I awoke on Friday to find that tongue had swollen to fill my entire mouth. It was most uncomfortable, I couldn't even put my front teeth together. On the downside this resulted in me being detained over the weekend, but on the plus side, Dr Barrowby advised me to eat only ice cream for the next few days. I enjoyed this, though I am beginning to tire of it a little now. Fortunately the swelling has been reduced, and I'm almost back to normal. Hopefully this will result in me being granted parole within the next few days.

I have now not left my room, let alone the hospital in nearly two weeks. The staff and visitors still have to wear masks upon entering, and I have become ambivalent to this. Out of my window I can see that the transition for Autumn to Winter has been completed, evidenced by the sharp morning frost. I imagine the cold winds will feel most alien to my central heating accustomed flesh when I do finally step outside. I worry that when I leave here I may be allergic to the world.

MONDAY 7TH DECEMBER 1998
Back inside again. Spent the best part of a week at home only for my killer headaches to return again. It's driving me crazy now; I can't remember

what it's like to be healthy. It's been three weeks since my last lumbar puncture and I still can't stand up for more than ten minutes at a time. In addition to this the time spent in a hospital bed has resulted in my leg muscles atrophying to the point where I find it uncomfortable to support my own weight. I am covered in sores and patches of dry skin, my neck aches, my gums bleed, and I keep falling asleep. The depressing part is not being able to make use of my time outside of hospital. Going home isn't much fun if you can't get out of bed for more than ten minutes in every hour. As usual the doctors' remedy for my ailments is more time in hospital and more infusions of blood. I don't see how this is going to stop my headaches.

In a rather tragic way, I can see some good in being back in hospital. I admit that when I'm at home I'm tempted to over exert myself and this results in my oft stated exasperation at my symptoms. At least in hospital I can relax and have some degree of peace and quiet. I'm worried that I may be becoming like the old people on the ward: Institutionalised. I may end up fearing the dangerous dirty world outside and start inventing complaints in order to spend more time in hospital. I'm suspicious of the old people here. They talk only amongst themselves, and in a language I can't understand. They are plotting against me.

WEDNESDAY 9TH DECEMBER 1998
So the doctors came round yesterday to assure me that some progress is being made on the mysterious cause of my headaches. Barrowby told me that a CT scan would be necessary to examine my brain and make sure everything is in order. This would be undertaken forthwith. So I spend today sitting about my room patiently awaiting the call that would summon me to the scanning room. By the evening nothing has happened, so I grab a passing nurse and ask if perhaps someone had forgotten to alert me to my appointment. Not so. It appears that the machine is in frequent use and as I am a low priority, I am effectively on 'standby', like with aeroplane tickets. No one knows when my scan will be, and no appointment can be made. I have just spent a whole day in hospital, and a good amount of taxpayers' money for no reason. In keeping with my lack of medical treatment, the telephone lies silent.

As I spend so much time indoors, and have a greatly reduced level of contact with other humans, I turn to the news media as my source of information regarding the outside world. Every day I read the *Guardian*, watch BBC1 (afternoon, evening and late bulletins) news, Channel 4 news, and usually *Newsnight* also. Although I believe myself to be a discerning, educated viewer, I cannot escape the suspicion that my impression of certain things is being skewed somewhat by the repetition of dominant news values in my daily intake. For example, due to the stories regarding their financial crisis, political instability, their Mafia, and the Chechnya kidnappings, I have developed a pathological fear of the former Soviet Union. Growing up in the eighties we were taught as western children that the USSR was a powerful and sinister super power – equal and opposite to the USA. In the nineties it has been transformed into an urban ghetto the size of a continent. It is the Bronx or Moss Side multiplied a million fold. Imagine a country where no one has a job, but everyone has a Kalashinakov. I had a dream on Monday night that I was a western businessman kidnapped by the Russian Mafia. My apologies to the Russian people for wishing never to visit their country.

SUNDAY 13TH DECEMBER 1998

I'm not having the best time ever. I woke up on Friday just knowing that I was going to be ill. A shower couldn't shake this grim clairvoyance, and I awaited the fateful moment. It came around 11am when I puked my liquid breakfast up into the toilet. This was accompanied by a splitting headache. I repeated this act a few hours later, but produced only sunflower yellow bile. Not pleasant. None of the doctors seemed too interested when I told them. The results of my CT scan came through and thankfully I am not suffering from any bleeding of the brain. I imagine this to be most unpleasant. This leads the doctors to the conclusion that my headaches are migraines. I'm not so sure as they occur whenever I stand up, and this is a rather unusual thing to be allergic to.

So they send me home on Saturday and true to form my headaches return. The pills prescribed by the doctors have no effect whatsoever. Can you imagine how depressing it is to not even be able to walk to the bathroom without an explosion of pain across the forehead? This gets me rather depressed as I spend the entire evening on the couch. I wake up on Sunday and resume my position there.

I've got to the point now where I can almost forget that I have leukaemia, as the headaches seem a more pressing concern. I hate to harp on about this, but an allergy to movement is a hard thing to bear. I have an appointment with Dr Tringham on Wednesday, and I'm going to press the issue as strongly as possible. I can't carry on like this. I haven't had chemotherapy in nearly a month now, and I've still got these hideous side effects. How much longer is this going to last?

TUESDAY 22ND DECEMBER 1998

So I'm back at home again, although I'm growing increasingly unsure of why this is. If it wasn't for the unpalatable nature of hospital catering, I'd be pleading to be re-admitted. I'm trapped in a vicious triangle with my headaches at the apex. The more recent attempts to relieve my symptoms have again proved fruitless, and I have also had to invest in my own drugs for these purposes. I knew the anti-migraine tablets wouldn't work; I still insist it's not migraines. Anyway in one of the brief periods in which I was able to stand, I took a short trip to buy some vodka (a gift) and some paracetemol. What does your shopping basket say about you?

So I've spent the last few days lying prostrate and indulging in less than high brow entertainment. For some reason at home I am pre-disposed to watch television rather than read or write. Watching television all day is very depressing, and the more I lie on the couch, the harder it is to leave. Lying on the couch all day to avoid headaches causes my neck and shoulders to ache and stabbing pains to shoot down my arms. I sit up to relieve the tension and my head aches. This is the second point of my vicious triangle, the third being the continual moan of my calves, which as I have mentioned before, have atrophied during my hospital tenure. Likewise, exercising my legs is difficult, due to the recurrence of my headaches.

I'm becoming like the old people who irritate me so on the ward – continually moaning about aches and pains. Well I never used to be a 'sick person', I hardly ever took days off school (for genuine reasons), and the same goes for my various terms of employment. Any days taken off for illness were either bogus or due to skateboard related injuries. I guess I'm using my quota of gripes and grumbles for the past twenty years now.

I am harvesting my own urine samples at present. This is necessary to check that my liver is functioning acceptably for the next phase of treatment[22]. In order to accomplish this, the hospital has equipped me with two plastic cartons which I have to fill over a 24 hour period. Quite literally a pot to piss in. It's such a dignified existence, having leukaemia. Tomorrow I'll carry a couple of litres of my own piss in bottles in a carrier bag to a hospital waiting room in which I will collapse due to various aches and pains. Someone will hopefully relieve me of that of which I have relived myself and then take some blood for good measure. Unfortunately the staff at Grantham hospital aren't qualified to take blood from Hickman lines, so they will have to use a syringe. I hate that – needles are

---

22 It's actually Jonathan's kidneys which are being checked.

everyday people with their everyday diseases. Professional patients have permanent pipelines.

TUESDAY 29TH DECEMBER 1998

What has happened in the last week? It was Christmas and I was at home which I guess was a good thing. I achieved complete remission on my bone marrow sample again which is good, and things generally went according to plan. Christmas was nice enough, and even my headaches relented to the festive atmosphere, hopefully for good. Dr Tringham also felt the need to prescribe me Prozac, which is interesting. I can't say I've really appreciated any effects yet though.

I can't really be bothered to write about Christmas week, I'm far more concerned with my present circumstances. I checked into the Hogarth Ward of Nottingham City Hospital today. I don't know why, but I always presumed it would be better for some reason. Perhaps it's the location; bigger city, better hospital. The location is better as well, much more accessible for my friends to visit me. Anyway, during my stay at Boston, I'd begun to picture Nottingham as some sort of Five Star medical facility, with luxurious rooms and beautiful nursing staff. This proved not to be the case.

My first impressions of the hospital were pleasant enough; it's an enormous complex, with many modern buildings. My suspicions were raised when we finally located the appropriate ward. It was (and is) a primarily open ward. That is to say – not individual rooms. After filling in some details I was led to a cluster of four beds in an area to the side of the main corridor. This was to be my new home. The three other occupants are an elderly man to my right, a very ill looking fellow of a similar age to myself opposite and right, and a rather healthy looking young teenager directly opposite. There is a communal television which seems to be permanently tuned to ITV. I doubt if my fellow inhabitants will share my fondness for *Newsnight*. Above the television is a pathetic attempt at Christmas decorations; it looks frailer than the patients.

I met my new doctors. They seem nice enough, but they chose to begin our relationship by completely contradicting everything that my original doctors said. It transpires that a bone marrow transplant from an unrelated donor was never an option, as the risk of death would be too great. I'm fucking gutted. Why was I led to believed that this was the preferred method of treatment? So I am forced to resign myself to two years of treatment. The doctors leave me, and I lie silent for a few hours to absorb this. This is not developing into one of my better days.

Later the nurses come round to fill me in on more practical details. The shower (singular please note) is right at the other end of the ward. There is one telephone. One phone for God knows how many patients. They don't know about internet access, but the idea sounds rather repellent to them. There's a phone jack by my bed, but they tell me it probably won't work. Great.

A guy I knew from Boston is here, and has been for three weeks. He assures me that the place does suck as much as I think it does.

TUESDAY 29TH DECEMBER 1998

I can't quite come to terms with how I feel about it all. Last week when I went with Jonathan on a clinic visit, I completely got the wrong end of the stick and became very irate when Dr Tringham said, 'Maybe you should offer him a little more support'. What else can I do? Fuss over him 24 hours a day? Follow him like a shadow and allow him no space or privacy? It's been one hell of a shock to all of us. I am not well versed in caring for cancer patients. They don't offer classes on this, you know.

I suppose I'm just plain tired. When was the last time that I slept for an eight-hour stretch? God knows. I usually sleep for about 3 hours, wander around the house for 2-3 more, and then fall asleep on the settee at about 4am. Even then it's a restless sleep, full of dreams that feel like being awake.

Dr Tringham feels that Jonathan may be a bit depressed and has prescribed him Prozac. I think under the circumstances he has been absolutely marvellous, strong and positive. I disagree with her decision.

Christmas has come and gone. Where?

Another new chapter begins with a visit to Nottingham City Hospital. This time the journey takes us along the A52 in the opposite direction. The road is a little straighter, but the journey time is still about 55 minutes, sometimes a little longer as we have to cross Nottingham. Still a long time to try and not think about things.

We enter the ward. I hate it. On sight. It's noisy, crowded and smells of urine and 'dinner'. We are asked to wait in the corridor. People, presum-

ably 'day patients', keep walking past. They seem like movie extras walking through the ward viewing the sick in their beds.

Eventually we are shown to a bay of four beds. Jonathan's is in the far corner. The television is on at full volume, competing with Radio Trent playing loudly in the corridor. The guy in the next bed is trying to talk to his visitors, the young lad in the opposite bed listens to his walkman on full volume, the chap in the other bed lies there moaning 'nurse, nurse, ohhhh, oh' and more. Basically I am a kind and caring person but I want to go to him and scream, 'Shut the fuck up!'

A random lady arrives with a pair of curtains. She grabs a chair and proceeds to try to hang them around Jonathan's bed while we're visiting. I stifle the desire to scream.

The doctor arrives. The discussion starts with another bombshell: Jonathan's bone marrow type is so rare that a transplant cannot be and never was a viable option! I try so hard not to cry, but I do. The tears continue to fall all the way home.

I do not want to leave my son in that hell hole, but somehow I have to.

WEDNESDAY 30TH DECEMBER 1998

The days drag on like fingernails on blackboards. After a largely sleepless night thanks to my neighbour's snoring, I was woken at 6am for the mandatory temperature and blood pressure checks. I must have fallen asleep again, because the next thing I knew it was 9am and someone was bitching for me to get out of bed. They threw us out and re-made the bed clothes. After an hour or so for breakfast they threw us out and re-made the beds again. And took the room to pieces. No, I don't mind if you unplug my computer, pour water over my minidisc player and drop my stuff on the floor.

My parents come over again but I'm in no mood to talk. On the plus side, my Dad finds a PC in the hospital where I can check my email. I send a few seasonal messages and return to my room, anxious not to overuse my new found privilege. Some genius has plugged a radio in the corridor just outside our 'bay'. It is tuned to a bad a local commercial station which plays the same 6 or 7 songs all day. This does not make me feel better, especially as one of them is Celine Dion and *that* song.

I started some chemotherapy today that made me tired and wishing to urinate often. The Doctor tells me that I probably can't leave until Saturday. That's three days and a whole new year away. I ask a nurse later if there is anywhere I can go to be alone. She simply shrugs and says, 'NHS'. I lock myself into the toilet and cry for a while, because there is nothing else to do.

THURSDAY 31ST DECEMBER 1998
Another bad day. Another early morning rise and depressing few hours before lunch. I can't eat anything, and even neglect to take my Prozac and steroids. Consequently I'm in a depressed, lackadaisical mood until around 2pm. I finally get round to taking my medicine and decide to go and check my email at the office round the corner. A sorry little note informs me that due to illness it will be closed until Monday. Marvellous. I then decide to watch a video. The VCR in our room has no rewind, so I have to go into another room to rewind my tape. When I return I find that our VCR will not play it. I am very depressed. I spend a good amount of time staring out of the window trying to ignore everyone else.

My Dad turns up a bit later and thankfully I'm disconnected from my drip for a while. This allows us to walk about the hospital grounds for a while, which is refreshing. I buy some food in the restaurant, but the sight of it makes me sick. We return to my room, and I'm exhausted. After my Dad leaves I stare at the clock for a while. The hands move excruciatingly slowly.

Later in the evening I hide in the staff training room, so that I can be alone. Eventually a nurse finds me and tells me that I need an injection. I return to my bed where an unfamiliar doctor waits to treat me. The injection is the most painful I have ever endured. Thankfully I don't have another scheduled until next week. When the curtains are drawn back I find that the young guy opposite has been replaced by an old fellow on a respirator. He looks like death, and I find this uncomfortable. I want to go home.

Tonight is New Year's Eve.

FRIDAY 1ST JANUARY 1999
Ah, fuck, my neck hurts! I don't know what I've done to it, but I can't keep my head up at the moment. My vision is kinda blurred too. I really can't see well at all. I don't want to tell the doctors in case this means that I have to stay in longer. Bastards! I'm completely touch typing now. I'm hot as well.

Another dull and depressing day in Nottingham City Hospital. When we were awoken at 6am, the nurse greeted us with 'Happy New Year!' I wanted to tell her to go fuck herself, but I'm too polite. The rest of the day was the normal drag, with the doctors assuring me that I will not be going home today. I have decided that tomorrow I will go home even if it means discharging myself. My eyesight appears to be returning, though.

The toilet stinks of old piss. I hate it.

The tragic result of living here means that I spend the whole day looking forward to bedtime. It's the only time when I'm alone (relatively speaking), have peace and quiet, and am less aware of the passage of time. It's 9.20pm now, and I'm counting away this last hour or so before lights out.

WEDNESDAY 6TH JANUARY 1999

So my brief sojourn at home had to come to an end. I wake at around 6am this morning as it is 'essential I make it to Hospital by 8.30am.' The cold morning air bites hard, and the sunrise clatters against the metallic bodywork of my dad's car. I compose myself for another stay in my least favourite hospital. By the time we get to Nottingham, I'm convinced that it was the shock of it all that upset me last time. I surprise myself with my optimism, but then again I took a double dose of Prozac this morning.

Things start going wrong about five minutes from the hospital, when I decide to throw up. Unfortunately I haven't had any breakfast, so it's pretty much pure bile. Unpleasant. And ominous.

It soon becomes apparent that I should have ignored the hospital's demand for me to arrive so early. I am not happy, I am fond of sleep. My Dad isn't happy either. I was supposed to be meeting the radiotherapy doctor this morning, in order for a protective mask to be fitted for my face. 'Morning' in hospital has varying meanings: 'Wake up it's morning' means two hours after bedtime, 'morning doctor's appointment' means sometime after lunch. My rendezvous with the Doc is eventually scheduled for 11.30am, I eventually see him at 12.30am, four hours after I was told to arrive. And what happened at this meeting? He told me that I needed a mask fitted for my face. To protect me from the radiotherapy. Yes, I understand, isn't this why I'm here? Oh no, we won't make the mask for a few weeks yet. You can go now.

My Dad is angry now. I tell him to go to work whilst I wait to see if there actually is a bed for me.

3.30pm: A bed is found. I have spent the afternoon sitting in the corridor.

9.30pm: I am writing this. I have received no treatment.

FRIDAY 8TH JANUARY 1999

So two fun, fun days in the hospital over with. They have been so uneventful that I feel it would be unfair of me to burden the reader with any account of their monotony. The one fairly interesting thing that happened today was that I had a plaster of Paris mould of my face made. This was in order to produce a plastic mask for my radiotherapy treatment. It was an unusual process, but not unpleasant. I don't feel I have anything more to say about the past 48 hours. That's how exciting it is here.

THURSDAY 14TH JANUARY 1999

Back at home again thank God. I swear that place was driving me insane, the days grinding round like sandpaper on my skin. I got home to find out that the Welfare Office have completely fucked up my benefits again, and I haven't got any money. They even gave me shit for not sorting it out myself! I'm also slightly depressed that the simple fact of being at home is not as thrilling as I thought it would be. Still, with the help of Nintendo and Sony, I'll get through it.

MONDAY 8TH FEBRUARY 1999

So I start the long-awaited radiotherapy today. I lie flat on a hard bench, my plastic mask bolted own so my head is rendered immobile. The machine hums and the air burns. I can feel my face prickling and a foul smell fills the air. Fortunately this only lasts for around thirty seconds. The process is then repeated for the other side of my head. Afterwards a nurse fills me in on the expected side effects. Aside from the usual stuff like hair loss, fatigue, rashes etc, I am upset to learn that I will have to wear a hat in the sun for the next two years. It seems like I'm never going to be normal again. Apparently the radiotherapy is like bad sunburn, and so I have to protect the targeted area from the elements.

In the afternoon I have the dreaded lumbar puncture. Today's is not made any easier by the presence of a doctor whose English skills are roughly equivalent to my medical skills. I am worried when she asks me if I have had any chemotherapy yet. Has she even read my files? I try and answer her questions as best I can, but she just nods vaguely at any answer I give, and I wonder if she understands a word I'm saying. She's adept enough with the needle though, and the injection itself is only as unpleasant as any that I've had before. I go home and throw up.

TUESDAY 9TH FEBRUARY 1999
More radiotherapy. I can feel the hairs on my arms pricking up as the machine hums into life. I can't stand the acrid smell that fills the air. I'm sick several times. When I get home I try to eat something, but I'm sick again. I'm so tired.

WEDNESDAY 10TH FEBRUARY 1999
I wake up around 12.30pm, still tired. The driver who's taking me today is wearing a different shoe on each foot, and has a crucifix Velcroed to the dashboard of his car. The radiotherapy is much the same as before and at least today I refrain from being sick. I even manage to eat a piece of toast, though this is the only food I've had in 48 hours.

THURSDAY 11TH FEBRUARY 1999
I make it to hospital OK, but I puke all over the car of the nice minicab bringing me home. Because I haven't eaten anything, it's pure yellow bile, running like lava across the seats, the floor. He's not too impressed.

FRIDAY 12TH FEBRUARY 1999
I must have got it out of my system, because I neither puke nor fall asleep today. I even consider going to Leicester to hang out with friends, but decide this would be pushing my luck. Halfway through my radiotherapy and apart from the sickness I'm doing OK. I noticed in the waiting room that none of the patients are bald or have red raw skin. Maybe the whole side effects thing is a myth or at least a worst case scenario. In the hospital I read *Country Life Magazine* and drool over ads for apartments overlooking Tower Bridge. £1 Million for a penthouse. The thing that sucks about leukaemia is you can't sue anyone for it. A nice compensation payout would help about now.

MONDAY 15TH FEBRUARY 1999
Monday is Lumbar Puncture Day, and that does not make me happy. Curled up embryo-like on the bed, I await my Doctor of Indeterminate Pacific Rim Origin to do her worst. She's trying to make conversation about the usual subjects – my degree, my choice of career. Unfortunately her English seems to have deteriorated even further, and my contribution to the conversation soon turns to vague murmurs of agreement. Undeterred, she plunges the needle into my spine and the dull throb of the anaesthetised process pulsates throughout my torso. As she reaches the end of the injection she withdraws the needle, but foolishly attempts to couple this with further attempts to engage me in conversation. The result of her divided attention is the agonising scrape of the needle against

one of my vertebrae. At this point I realise that the needle must have penetrated some one and a half inches into my spine. As usual I spend the afternoon and evening staring at the ceiling, my poor tortured spine moaning at me.

THURSDAY 18TH FEBRUARY 1999
The week has been rather mundane to be honest. My body appears to have grown accustomed to the radiotherapy, which produces very few side effects at the moment. I've only been sick once this week, which is about a dozen times less than last. Tomorrow is my final radiotherapy session, and then I have only one phase of chemotherapy left. I am beginning to see the fabled light at the end of the tunnel.

FRIDAY 19TH FEBRUARY 1999
My final radiotherapy session! Thankfully it all goes to plan and the doctor confirms that I am free to leave the world of radiotherapy hell. In celebration my brother drags me into Nottingham City centre where I blow a hundred quid's worth of taxpayer's money on a new pair of Nikes and some records.

SUNDAY 21ST FEBRUARY 1999
So I've had an enjoyable weekend with friends in Nottingham and Leicester. On Sunday evening I drive back from Leicester to Grantham. In the car I'm thinking to myself how I'm starting to live a rather more normal life at the moment, and that before long it'll all be over. Fate must have heard my complacency as all of a sudden the heavens opened and the road was blanketed with snow. I slowed down, but when I turned into a sharp bend on a steep hill, the car carried on in a tragically straight line. I flew straight out of the corner, down a ditch and into a tree. Shit.

Strangely, my first thoughts were to turn off the music and change from my spanking white Nikes into my old Emericas. My car may be ruined but there's no point trashing a brand new pair of sneakers. So I crawl out of the ditch and flag down a lorry driver over who gave me a lift back home and the use of his mobile to call the Police. At 2am, me and my Dad meet the tow truck and watch as they winch my poor Mum's new car out of the snow-filled gully. The damage wasn't too bad actually, could have been a lot worse. Hey I'm a survivor – cancer and a car crash, all in one year!

MONDAY MARCH 8TH 1999
So I've been out of hospital for a few weeks, off medication, and just for

a while I could forget that this whole thing ever happened. Unfortunately when I shower my Hickmann line is always there to remind me[23], and when I run my hand across my barren scalp it all comes home.

But it all returned to business as usual today when I returned to Boston Hospital for me final stage of chemotherapy. That it's the final stage is a good thing, but the duration is somewhat longer than I anticipated. It looks as if my treatment will extend until July, which is demoralising to say the least. The three months ahead actually contain very little treatment, and I'm grateful for the fact that I will not spend too much time in hospital. On the other hand, spending two weeks at home is less fun than one would imagine: I have very few friends in Grantham, and the house is always empty.

I was almost excited to return to Boston today after my displeasure at Nottingham's facilities. I was happy to see the friendly nursing staff, and the private rooms which appear palatial compared to Nottingham's open wards. It soon wore off as I moved my stuff into a very noisy room, thank you very much, and realised that the menu had still not changed, three months on. The three Mohammeds have sadly left, and Antonio is nowhere to be seen. Denton is still his cheerful self, which is far preferable to the stand-offish attitude of the Nottingham doctors. I'm watching TV, a shaky picture, typing my diary; it feels as if the last three months never happened.

TUESDAY MARCH 9TH 1999
Last night was a bit of a struggle. See I got assigned the room right next to the nurses' station, which means 24-hour commentary. Also my curtains don't fit, and even if they did they're practically translucent so they wouldn't be too much help. Thankfully they managed to supply me with some illicit drug or other that knocked me right out. Amazingly they let me sleep in as well (perhaps as an apology for keeping me awake till 2am), so that wasn't too bad.

The day was pretty uneventful. I watched the budget speech and then went for dinner with my folks in the evening. I had a few beers, so it feels like I'm typing uphill. I tumble every time I hit 'pgdn' by mistake. This is too tiring.

WEDNESDAY MARCH 10TH 1999
Another uneventful day. One of the nurses, Bev, is a terrible flirt, and this

---

23 It's a common difficulty of patients with Hickmann lines to undress in front of others because of the self-consciousness of the line.

provides some distraction for the day. I spend the afternoon trying to think of designs for a new tattoo, and I watch terrible television programmes. I fear that this diary is going to be rather dull from henceforth. None of my treatment seems to contain any drama anymore. Perhaps I should attempt to contract some infection or other in order to provide a new twist to this tale.

THURSDAY MARCH 11TH 1999

Uneventful again. It looks as if the next three weeks are going to be pretty barren of treatment which I guess is a good thing. However, no-one calls and few email. I 'm sick of doing nothing the time. It's so hard to be motivated in a hospital room. I hate to say this, but I think I need college, or a job to give me some direction. I want to be normal again.

SUNDAY MARCH 14TH 1999

I spend the weekend fuelled by steroids, drinking and eating far too much. In Lincoln, some charity people photograph me as 'Lincoln's Baldest Man', which is quite amusing. I haven't got any real treatment this week, just a two minute injection which I have to travel all the way to Boston for. Thankfully my car has now returned from the garage after I crashed it the other week. I guess this diary's going to start getting real sparse, as I don't spend that much time in hospital anymore. Mind you I still spend just enough to make a 'normal' life impossible. I'm now facing the problem where I have a lot of time on my hands, but only a very limited source of income. And with no friends in Grantham, I'm inclined to pass the time through commerce.

I'm still ill though, so don't stop your sympathy yet. I'll keep you posted if anything exciting happens.

TUESDAY 6TH APRIL 1999

So, three weeks on from my last entry, and I'm back in for another five day stretch. As this happened to fall over Easter, I have to be admitted Tuesday to Saturday as opposed to the more traditional Monday to Friday, in order to allow the staff some reprieve on the Holy Day. The fact that 75% of the staff here are obviously not Christian appears irrelevant.

I get here at 11am, just as they asked, in order for me to be in time for their scheduled chemotherapy. As usual however, it transpires that a room will not be available until 3pm. I'm connected up to my drip in the corridor, but the battery on the pump runs out so they have to put me in one of the storage rooms so I can reach a power point. The connector leaks as well, and I get chemicals all over my hands and clothes. I love being back in hospital.

28 days of high dose steroids have not been kind to me. Aggravated by tedium I consumed foodstuffs voraciously during my time at home, and paid the price. Unfortunately the treatment's effect on my appetite was not matched by any increase in energy, so the calories hung on for dear life. The doctors and nurses noticed, as have my friends and family, but I guess I'm allowed to be fat for once. Sobolovski's words 'he now looks menacing, though less like a skeleton' were apt enough I guess. With my bald head and fattened face I've got that Ernst Blofeld / Dr Evil kind of thing going on.

Important note: The phone line in this room does not allow me to make outgoing calls at the moment. This is a problem, as I cannot retrieve my email. I will not be reduced to the level of a caveman. They have until lunchtime tomorrow to remedy it, or heads will roll! Oh, but I do hate to complain...

THURSDAY 8TH APRIL 1999

Oh my! Such excitement. I had obviously been a little presumptuous expecting all my treatment to go without a hitch from now on. I awake at 3am convinced I am dead (the result of a dream). I'm basting in sweat and consumed by one of those agonisingly generic sicknesses. I hit the 'panic' button and 10 minutes later an orderly looks in. She goes off to find a nurse who arrives 15 minutes later. She says she needs to get a doctor. He arrives an hour later. The doctor says he needs to take some blood. He sends for a different nurse to do this. She arrives 15 minutes later. I'm angry because she sticks a needle in my arm instead of using my Hickmann line. The blood is taken away. I get some antibiotics at 5am, by which time I'm feeling kind of better anyway. The main result of my ordeal is that I hardly get any sleep. I'm woken at 7.30am.

I spend the afternoon willing myself to be better, because I definitely want to be out for Tony's birthday on Saturday night. It seems to work and I'm feeling OK by teatime. Infuriatingly my temperature, which had dropped during the afternoon to a respectable level, is higher in the evening, even though I feel far finer. The temperature is all that matters to the doctor, and I wish I knew some kind of yogic exercise for lowering it. I've got two days to make the grade, so fingers crossed.

I also fell victim to my own stupidity with my email, and picked up 37 errant messages, many months old. Tomorrow will, I envisage, involve a lot of writing.

FRIDAY 9TH APRIL 1999

I've left this a little too late, and I'm really tired but I feel I ought to make up for writing nothing yesterday. The past two days have seen my temperature fluctuate with ridiculous amplitude. Earlier this evening I was at a perfectly respectable 36.5 for an hour (after an hour at the only mildly high 37.2) when all of a sudden I rocketed to the insane 38.6[24]. I really can't see myself getting out tomorrow. What is it with people's 25th's? I missed Jay's, and I'm going to miss Tony's. If anyone is 25 soon, don't bother inviting me to your party.

The cause of my infection is still unknown. I had a chest X Ray which showed nothing and the doctors ordered an ECG. I asked Barrowby and Denton why, and the patronising fuckers (Denton particularly) just pulled baby faces and said 'heart'. Jesus Christ! They wouldn't volunteer any other information and just left the room. I was, needless to say, furious. Fortunately a friendly junior doctor filled me in on the details, and I voiced my complaints.[25]

SATURDAY APRIL 10TH 1999

Today was particularly unusual. At first I was tempted to be far more superlative in describing it, but from my experience the phrase 'it was so surreal' in anything other than an artistic context is far too often the catchphrase of someone incredibly tedious or stupid.. I'm hoping to capture of much of it as possible.

The story actually begins immediately after I saved the diary entry you have just read, took care of necessities and went to bed. My sleep was as it has been all week, far from normal. My dreams have been an insane collage of random images, sounds and actions. Completely devoid of any discernible narrative. A pure exercise in post-modernist kitsch. They were punctuated by several brief awakenings, though these contained

[*Entry breaks off here.*]

MONDAY APRIL 11TH 1999

No, you aren't missing any of the diary. I'll explain. On Saturday I

---

24 Common symptoms of an infection.
25 It's not uncommon for the source of such an infection never to be found.

became quite ill. The above entry is, I believe evidence of this. The day was particularly unusual because I now realise that I was quite delusional. In the morning I was pretty much OK, I even managed to change my hospital room to one with a working telephone line – hurrah! However, once I was settled in my new room the problems began.

My temperature rose to very high levels; the afternoon through to the evening saw me hover around the 38 degrees mark, sometimes as high as 38.8 (apologies to those more familiar with Fahrenheit[26]). I was in a quite a state mentally. As you probably know from reading this journal, I read the paper every day. I started reading it just after I'd settled into my new room and didn't finish reading it until I wrote Saturday's entry at around 11pm. My only other activities were a few phone calls and eating. I barely took any of it in, only the amusing articles in the supplements. The reason it took so long is that I was continually drifting off into bizarre daydreams, or simply staring at the wall for five minutes. I did snap out it when people entered the room and I pulled myself together, likewise when I spoke to people on the phone. By the evening, however, I really was in a terrible state. I wrote what I could of my diary then realised I couldn't go on. I decided to go to bed. The next thing I did was to write in my notebook: 'Written in a moment of lucidity. Tell (the names of some friends) and docs about this tomorrow'. I then took off my shirt, walked to the sink, and everything went wrong.

As I approached the sink I suddenly felt a bit tired and moved over to the chair next to it. Simultaneously a nurse, Leslie, entered the room with my pills. At that moment I fainted. Leslie caught me and lowered me into the chair. I came round, tried to talk and began vomiting. Not a huge amount, but enough. I was staring wildly. I was completely disorientated. The room was exploding around me. Leslie, with assured professionalism, calmed me down, and I began to explain what happened. A few sentences in I vomited again and snapped back in to delirium. Leslie began to ask a question, and I just interrupted with my answer ' YES YES YES YES', with no idea what she was asking. She managed to stop me and I began to calm again.

By this time a couple of support workers had turned up. I was pretty stable now. Leslie and a support worker began to clear the immediate area of the room, as they would have to move me to my bed without injuring me on any of the furnishings and other bits and pieces. The first thing to go

---

26 38C is approximately 100.5F, 38.8C is approximately 102F.

was the table with my computer. This has always been a point of consternation with the staff because it always has loads of wires trailing from it, and it's anchored to the power point and often the phone line. So moving it in an emergency is a nightmare. I watched as they frantically tried to move it, ripping out leads, thankfully they asked if they would damage anything, and I was able to direct them as to how not to. They got quite frustrated as plugs tangled, stuff fell off and general trouble ensued. It got done however, and pretty soon I was transferred to bed.

Once there I was soon joined by my favourite junior doctor, Dr Alapati (I kept forgetting his name for ages). I ran through what happened, and he conducted a few tests. I slipped a few times: when asked to open my eyes, I opened my mouth. When asked to look into his eyes, I rolled my eyes to the top of my head. Once the tests were done and some medication dispensed, I was allowed to sleep.

I awoke on Sunday, relieved that my harrowing ordeal was over. Naturally I spent the day in bed relaxing. I found myself weak and unsteady on my feet, but more worryingly I found that I still could not concentrate whilst reading. Likewise my conversations were a little fractured. I'm having trouble remembering much about Sunday, perhaps because I did try and do as little as possible. My parents visited.

So. Today. My concentration is improving, but it's still not there completely. I suppose this has implications for the content of this entry, but I feel I must get this written down now or I'll never catch up with events. Today I had a 24 hour heart monitor attached to me. It's like a walkman with 6 wires attached by stickers to my chest. Nice and comfortable for sleeping tonight then. I presumed it would be an audio recording of my own heart, which is then analysed by computer for whatever it is they look for. I was gutted when I asked if I could keep the tape. Unfortunately the cassettes, which look exactly like audio cassettes, will not play in a conventional stereo, and it's not an audio recording anyway. Gutted.

Aside from that, not too much has happened today. Oh, yes it has! My temperature has dropped to sensible levels and stayed there. I was in the 36.5 – 37.3 range all day. Looking good! I'm having some blood now and thinking of freedom.

11 APRIL 1999
Easter gone already. Must have joined Christmas in a joint mystery disappearance.

We decide to go away to London for the weekend to have a break. Jonathan is in the local hospital receiving routine chemo. His brothers and our many friends are on standby just in case. So, it's a day or two for me and Peter to relax, to do touristy things, see the sights, go to the theatre. Our caravan is well equipped, a home from home, and we dare to 'switch off' for a bit, pretend the rest of the world isn't happening.

Things go well until the Sunday morning phone call.

*   'Hi son, ok?'*
*   'Fine thanks, had a bit of a bad night.'*

PANIC! We're over 100 miles away! I pack the caravan in record time and we're off, charging up the A1. Yet another 'drama'. Will we make it? We tell ourselves the usual things: He's a fighter, keep positive.

The journey drags; the caravan is slow. The A1 stretches endlessly before us. We both stare ahead. Finally, after three hours, the hospital. I still can't remember what we did with the caravan, but I do recall that we never paid to park the car. We didn't have the change.

I run to the ward, my heart in my mouth, hell happening in my head. MY SON! Was he still alive? I burst in through the door.

*   'Hi Mum. What are you doing here? I'm OK now.'*

I'm his mum, so I suppress the need to scream and bang my head against the wall. Instead, I gently kiss him on the forehead/

After racing up the A1, Peter and I spend most of the time discussing the film we saw last night Shakespere in Love, of all things. We also describe at length our visit to The Tower of London. It is truly amazing how many alternative topics of conversation you can come up when you don't want to talk about cancer.

Jonathan casually mentions that the doctor on duty the previous evening had not 'experienced' a patient undergoing chemo before, nor had he been party to the possible side effects of the treatment, which was why Jonathan had been feeling sicker than normal. But a quick phone call to Dr Tringham had confirmed that what was happening was totally manageable, and the new doctor had followed her instructions to the letter. Jonathan was concerned for the guy: 'It shook him up a bit, Mum". Not one mention of what might have been.

He's still here and hanging on in there... Keep going son.

SATURDAY APRIL 16TH 1999

Another large gap, again due to illness. OK here we go. On Tuesday I was discharged from Boston with the proviso that I visit Grantham Hospital each day for a six-hour drip to clear out my fungal infection (in my blood). This was to last for two weeks, which sucks a bit, but at least I was going home each evening. Unfortunately I almost immediately registered a temperature and was kept in over night. Argh! By the evening I was actually feeling ill, and I resigned myself to another long stay.

Wednesday I basically slept through. There were medicines and nurses and family involved, but mostly I just slept. Likewise Thursday, but I was a little more awake. The doctors decided to transfer me to Boston. I didn't mind this, although it meant saying goodbye to an extremely beautiful junior doctor who'd been looking after me.

So yesterday I arrived at good old Pilgrim Hospital. I was brought here on a stretcher in an ambulance, which seemed rather dramatic, but I didn't mind. Gradually starting to feel better, but I still had flu-like symptoms, and I was still really tired. I hate being ill, it sucks. One worrying development was that the blood taken from my Hickmann line showed infection, and this could lead to the line being removed prematurely. This is quite an unlikely event though, but it did concern me somewhat.

So today I'm feeling quite a bit better. I did still have to have a good nap in the afternoon, but as you can see I've finally mustered the energy to write this diary. One really annoying symptom that still persists is an acid taste in my mouth which makes it hard to eat or drink. I don't have much of an appetite anyway, but this makes things worse. Here's to continued improvement...

MONDAY 19TH APRIL 1999

A marked improvement over the last two days. Yesterday I took the important step of getting out of bed at a reasonable time and dressing for the day. I was noticeably unsteady on my feet, nearly killing myself stepping out of the shower, but I felt good for making the effort. I still had to have a nap (2 hours) in the afternoon.

A similar story today. Only one hour of napping required so far, and I've finally shaken off that hideous acid taste. I've also regained my appetite which is good for my recovery, but when I wasn't eating at least I didn't have to consider hideous hospital food. I haven't seen a consultant in ages, so I've no idea how much longer I'm going to be here. Apparently I'm low on potassium so I'm receiving supplements in both pill and drip form. Luckily I also have a bunch of bananas with me, which is an odd coincidence.

TUESDAY 20TH APRIL 1999

One hour of napping this morning. I long for an uninterrupted night's sleep. For some reason my treatment is arranged to cause maximum disruption to my slumber. I can't remember the last time I slept continuously through the night. In the afternoon the doctors came round to tell me that despite the fact that I feel fine and my temperature is stable, I would still have to remain in hospital until at least the end of the week. I'm pretty pissed off. I spend enough time in hospital as it is without these stupid infections, and I'd probably be a hell of a lot better if I could go home and get some decent rest!

THURSDAY 22ND APRIL 1999

Yesterday saw me adventure into the darkest depths of the hospital as I was ferried to the echo-cardiogram and CT departments. On the way I saw many wretched souls, abandoned in corridors, despairing eyes staring back at me. The tests were mundane enough, but the CT scan was a little tortuous as I had to keep my hands above my head for the duration. This accomplished, the rest of the day passed without incident.

Today I received the results of the CT which thankfully was clear. This means that the treatment for my fungal infection should only last two weeks, and not the feared six. No report on the echo yet, but I'm working on the 'no news is good news' principle'. Once more, the rest of the day was uneventful. Hoping that tonight might be slightly more peaceful. Dr Tringham thinks I may be able to return home after the weekend. I was hoping she was going to say tomorrow. The decision is apparently Barrowby's, and he isn't around until... tomorrow of course.

FRIDAY 23RD APRIL 1999

So I await the arrival of Dr Barrowby, and news my imminent or otherwise release. I kill most of the afternoon by sleeping, and wake just as the doctors begin massing at my door. I'm expecting news about my infection, but Barrowby springs a surprise. Apparently a near perfect donor has been found for me in Wales. I was unaware that they were still looking. I ask

Barrowby if it's really an option as Professor Russell at Nottingham was opposed to me having any kind of unrelated transplant. Barrowby (who is far nicer these days) assures me that with such a good match, this will not be the case. I'm confused by the whole thing. I'd resigned myself to not having a transplant, and this upsets my whole mindset about things. I've decided to avoid thinking about it until I have more information.

SATURDAY 24TH APRIL 1999

Another day and another turnabout in policy. Dr Tringham informs me that, just as I suspected, Nottingham are still not prepared to undertake an unrelated transplant for me. I'm not too bothered – I hate Nottingham, as you know. Still, at least I can take comfort in the knowledge that if I relapse, a donor is available. Other news from Dr Tringham is that she thinks my Hickmann line should be removed as they're only supposed to be in the body 3 months (mine's been in 6)[27]. She assures me that I don't have much treatment left, so it shouldn't mean too many needles instead, but we'll have to see. It'll certainly mean a needle in the arm every time I have a blood test.

MONDAY 26TH APRIL 1999

Finally! Freedom from Boston. I do have to return to my routine of visiting Grantham Hospital everyday, but let's hope it goes a little better than last time.

THURSDAY 6TH MAY 1999

Just an update to let you know where I'm at. So I began having my treatment at Grantham and it appeared to go well at first. I slept throughout most of it, which was nice. On Friday, though, things once again took a turn for the worse. I was sitting in my room receiving my medication when a doctor ran in and rather hurriedly disconnected me. It transpired that my kidneys were being damaged by the treatment, and I was facing possible renal failure. Nice. So I had to return to the hospital everyday for blood tests to check that my kidneys weren't collapsing.

Yesterday's results show that they've made improvements, but they're still a bit shaky. The real downside of all this is that either the medication or the reduced kidney function has left me with that hideous sour taste in my mouth again. I can't eat anything, not even pizza! Imagine how distressing this is. So at the moment I'm on a fruit diet, as apples, pears and

---

27 A possible misunderstanding, as Hickmann lines can be left in longer than three months.

pineapple appear to be the only things I can swallow. Hopefully this will be remedied soon. I've already lost a lot of weight, and I'm convinced it's not doing good things for my digestive system.

SATURDAY 15TH MAY 1999

So on Wednesday I went to see the dietician, which was far more productive than I thought it would be. She managed to advise me of ways to sustain myself without making myself violently sick, which was becoming a bit of a problem. Then I had an appointment with Dr Tringham, who talked through the next stage of my treatment. It seems that the term 'flexible' actually means they can make it last longer but not much else. It becomes apparent that meeting my target of June 29th (my birthday) for the end of my chemotherapy is not likely. I'm upset, but there's nothing I can do about it. I have some chemo and go home. Fortunately being able to eat again cheers me up.

On Thursday of course things go sour again. I find myself trapped all day in bed, unable to move. I eat a solitary cracker and resign myself early on to not making the Fugazi show that evening. As the day progresses, I feel worse, and I reluctantly check my temperature. One phone call, and I'm back in Boston Hospital.

Friday was not pleasant. I was very ill, the TV reception sucks, I'm not eating or drinking. I'd prefer to just forget about it.

I woke up today and despite having next to no sleep last night it appears the antibiotics are working. By the afternoon I'm feeling positively chipper, so I sprain a muscle in my neck to make up for it.

I received an application form for the *Guardian* Festival for Television and Young People in Edinburgh. Long serving readers may recall that this was the occasion last year that marked the onset of my symptoms. It brought home how desperately long this whole process has been. I decide to re-apply, as I will be ineligible next year. When the organisers ask me what I've been doing since the last festival, I want to be able to say 'I had leukaemia, but I'm better now'.

SUNDAY 16TH MAY 1999

Feeling better today, but as it's Sunday and there are no doctors around, nothing can be done about this. I am moved to a room which promises to have better TV reception. It does, but the phone line doesn't work. I'm moved again to a third room which has an OK picture and a working phone line. It's also the noisiest room due to its proximity to the Nurses' station. I wasn't even that bothered about the TV.

WEDNESDAY 19TH MAY 1999
Monday passed without event. The doctors came round on Tuesday, and as I had completed a course of antibiotics and felt fine, I figured they'd release me. Not so, further observation is required, and it could be Thursday or Friday before they see fit to grant me my freedom. The other topic of discussion was the Hickmann line, which is blamed as the source of my infections. It therefore has to be removed, and another put in.

Fine, if it's infected it has to go, but is another necessary? See, if they put in a second, it has to go on the other side of the chest. As each line leaves two penny shaped scars, the effect would be four corners of a rectangle across my chest. I wanted to know whether I could finish my treatment using peripheral veins. It's an option I was told, but it would result in a great deal of discomfort. What really annoyed me was Barrowby scream-ing 'scars are the least of your worries, you're lucky to be alive!' True, but I resent being made to feel guilty about retaining my quality of life after treatment. I've already got infertility as a souvenir, I don't need scarifica-tion.

Anyway, fuck it, today I decided to go ahead with it. All I can think about is how crap everything is as the sun shines through my window, burning me.

THURSDAY 20TH MAY 1999
Of course they changed their minds. So I'm going home now to return next Wednesday. I will then have my line removed, and we will use veins in my arm for the remainder of the treatment.

FRIDAY 28TH MAY 1999
The line came out on Wednesday, as promised. That was not fun. Going into it I was worried about the local anaesthetic injection most of all, as it was going to be directly into my left pectoral. Now I'm no athlete, but there's not a lot of fat around there, and I figured it was probably going to hurt quite a bit. It came as a pleasant surprise when Dr Denton per-formed the task, because I didn't even feel the needle go in. With the area suitably numb he began the process of removing the line.

Imagine if you will a plastic tube about the diameter of a drinking straw. Around this is a 'cuff' made of fabric, about 1 cm long. This cuff was left below the surface of the skin so that the surrounding tissue would grow into it. Dr Denton had to cut this apart and then pull out the line. Now the problem with my line is that it's been in my body for far longer than is recommended by the manufacturers. Therefore the tissue was particularly well attached to the line. I could hear the sound of his scissors cutting at the cuff and my flesh, and I could see the piles of blood soaked gauze mounting on his operating table. He soon began to tug at the line, at first tentatively, but soon he was yanking with all his strength. Each time he pulled it felt as if he was trying to take one of my ribs with him. I could feel shockwaves all through my chest, but they were a strange dull sensation due to the anaesthetic. Eventually with a spurt of blood the line came clear and we could all relax. I now have a small hole in my chest that will heal into a scar 'not unlike a bullet wound' or so I'm told.

Since then I've returned home, been a little bit sick but feeling OK now. Next Wednesday I can look forward to chemotherapy via needles in the arm! Lovely.

FRIDAY JUNE 4TH 1999
I'm now having my chemotherapy the old fashioned way, through a needle. This isn't that bad really. I'm so blasé about needles after nearly a year of this shit. The only real upset this week is that my haemoglobin fell to 6 so I required a blood transfusion[28]. I was given the option of two 6-hour stretches on consecutive days or a one-night stop 6pm – 6am flow. I took the overnight option. This was in retrospect a mistake: the room opposite mine housed a 'screamer' and I got no sleep. All night his bone rattling cries punctured the air and prevented me from slumber.

As I stumbled around the ward this morning, complaining about my fatigue, an annoyingly cheery nurse chipped in with 'you can see the light at the end of the tunnel now Jonathan'. I've been staring at this light for months now. It never seems to get any closer, and my eyes are beginning to hurt.

TUESDAY 8TH JULY 1999
Wow, a whole month since my last diary entry. Well I figured you wouldn't have been particularly interested in how I managed to watch practically every Wimbledon game and generally lounged about the house. I'm hoping that as my treatment draws to a close, the need for this diary will lessen. Next week I begin my final week of treatment. That hopefully

---

28 A normal haemoglobin count is 12–14.

should provide the material for my final entry, and I can draw this stage of my life to a close.

I haven't had any treatment these past two weeks due to a gap in the schedule, and my blood counts being a little low. This required yet another infusion of blood, which was conducted with farcical incompetence by the Grantham hospital staff. To cut a long story short, it resulted in pints of blood being spilt all over the floor at 1am. I don't really wish to relive the episode in this diary or elsewhere.

The good news is that my appetite has returned, and I'm gradually building my strength back up. The only visible side effect of my treatment is the ugly bruises from needles that adorn my hands and forearms. Even those are fading (though I'm sure next week's treatment will deliver a fresh batch).

So I'm here at home, collecting my welfare cheques and planning my holiday. I've also decided to make a clean break from my life pre-leukaemia, and I've made an application to transfer my university studies to London, Greenwich University. I'm expecting a decision from those in charge tomorrow. For this reason I decided to write this today, as I may be too depressed tomorrow. Let's hope not; I gave them the whole sob story about my illness so maybe they'll take pity.

Generally I'm feeling a lot happier. I really can see the end of this hellish year, and even now I'm starting to get out and enjoy myself more. I've been to some great gigs, been out with friends, and I turned 21 last week. OK so being 20 is going to go down as the worst year of my life. It's going to take something pretty fucking crap to make 21 any worse.

MONDAY 26TH JULY 1999
On Saturday the 24th of July I had the final dose of chemotherapy in my treatment schedule. I had been attending hospital each day for the week preceding, and Saturday marked the last instalment. This therefore marks the end of my treatment and the end of 'my war'. I will now be going on to a maintenance programme of taking pills and occasional injections, but for the most part I will be living as a normal healthy human being again (if I could just stop smoking!).

It's hard to know what to say really. It seems like an eternity since I was diagnosed with this illness. I really have had the worst year of my life, but you know all the details from reading my diary, so I won't go retread old ground. As I've mentioned in both this epistle and other writings I feel it has made me a stronger person, but I guess others will be the judge of that.

For once I'm really at a loss for words here. I thought this moment would be accompanied by reams of gushing prose, but I think now I'm ready to lay 'my war' to rest. Thank you to you all for your support, thank you for your friendship. I could not have done this alone.

JULY 1999

Jonathan has always talked of taking 'a year out' while at Uni. He wanted to travel, but instead he's spent most of the last year in a hospital bed undergoing chemotherapy, which naturally makes him even more determined to get out there and experience life. Chemo, as far as he is concerned, has been a total inconvenience, but he's now in remission. The outlook is positive.

For my part, I'm relieved to return to some sense of normality. After eighteen months of being tied to hospitals, it's suddenly strange to be able to choose what to do during the evening or at weekends.

The house is a tip, the garden a mess. What's also changed is that I simply don't care. Deep inside I still stifle the desire to scream. I have suppressed my feelings, bottled them up, kept them on hold, afraid to let go in case I completely lose control.

Everyday life has taken on a different perspective. When colleagues discuss issues at work I find myself thinking 'Does it really matter? Will the world come to an end because you haven't done your lesson plans on a certain format?' If I had it to do all over again, I wouldn't have continued working. The stress was too great.

One issue in particular called my judgement into question. I had spent hour upon hour supporting one particular student working under the supervision of a training provider. Many evenings I was torn between visiting Jonathan or continuing with her training and assessment. It was difficult to find a balance, but I worked hard at it. Then one day the student was supervising a very messy painting activity. After scrubbing four dirty pupils in a row, I suggested that the activity was cleared away. At the end of the day I talked to the student, explaining that the activity had not been up to the necessary standard and that she really must put more thought into what was expected of her. Her response to this was to report me to her" college". I was called to the Head's office. The student had raised a formal complaint against me! I managed to hold my cool until I left the room. The self-centred little cow! All that time! All that effort! The FIRST time I ask her to repeat an activity and this is her response! God, how I could slap her smug little face!

What was funny was that deep down I felt more angry and hurt about what she had done to me than about Jonathan having Leukaemia. Leukaemia was one of those terrible things that happen, something that you deal with as best you can, something that you put your energies into defeating rather than moaning about. I can accept that. What I can't accept is a student blaming me for her shortcomings. Funny how that works.

Still, back to Jonathan. He wasn't entirely free of hospitals, still having to report regularly to outpatient clinics. Each and everyday he still has to take copious amounts of medication. So many drugs, in fact, he usually returns from each appointment with a large carrier bag full of medication! He's also been given a card to carry which states that he is undergoing treatment for cancer and therefore has various drugs and substances on his person. We all treat this as a bit of a joke until one evening he drives home from Leicester in my car and is stopped by the police.

> *'Is this your vehicle Sir?'*
> *'No.'*

For no other reason than that he looks gaunt from the chemo (and therefore like a drug addict), the vehicle is searched.

> *'Are these for your own use, sir?'*
> *'Yes.'*
> *'What, ALL of them?'*
> *'Er, yes, I have cancer. Here's my card.'*

For some strange reason we all find this episode quite amusing.

And now, at last, the long summer holidays are finally upon us. Jonathan takes a long-planned trip to the USA and, much to Dr Tringham's horror, has planned a short excursion into Mexico. No one, least of all me, can dissuade him. 'They have hospitals there, too, yes I'll wear my sun hat, yes, I'll take it easy.' And so on. But, I still worry. Of course.

He's also decided to return to university to complete his degree. After much thought he opts to finish his course at Greenwich. He secures en-suite accommodation to prevent possible infections. He also has a meningitis jab, just in case. There will be distance between us, but its only in miles. As my dad always used to say, 'When you love them, you let them go.' Which, I suppose, is true even if they have cancer.

Jonathan's care has been transferred to Greenwich Hospital.

Things are going well.

SEPTEMBER 1999
Time to take a deep breath and start all over again with a new academic year. I tidy my classroom, update the paper work and plan the future. The days quickly settle into a familiar pattern: get up, work, shopping, washing, ironing, evening meal, phone calls/television/night class, relax, bed. 'Life' has returned to 'normal'. It's a good feeling.

We take Jonathan to the University Campus. It's modern, well-equipped and bright. A marked contrast to some of the hospitals he's been in. His accommodation consists of a private bedroom with en suite facilities and a shared kitchen/lounge area. The unit is mixed, its inhabitants have never met each other before and none are aware of Jonathan's medical history.

Amazingly, during his first lecture, Jonathan is asked to write about what it would feel like to be told that you have cancer. Then his first night he's kept awake by the constant abuse that two rival groups of students hurl at each other out on the campus. He goes to make a drink only to discover that the shared kitchen area is dirty, the fridge contains some "suspect" items and the bin is overflowing. It all proves too much. He returns to his room and throws a chair at the wall.

'Mum, help!' I listen patiently. His immediate reaction is to leave Uni. 'Come on, son. you've only got a few months until you get your degree. You'll do it.' I suggest that he speaks to his tutor, talks to his flat mates, talks to me. I really want to rush down there and put it all right for him – he's still my child even though he's a grown man. Several days later he calls me. He has addressed most of the issues with his flatmates and is going to attend counselling with an emphasis on anger management. He says it's the ferocity of his own anger frightened him. All that bottled-up rage at the leukaemia. I replace the receiver and weep.

I find myself weeping again a few weeks later: David (Jonathan's 19-year-

old brother) has entered The Great North Run. He dislikes needles and hospitals, but wants to do something. Peter and I wave him off at the start. It's an extremely emotional experience watching all those thousands of people run by. We finally reached the finish at South Shields (Getting there by public transport was it's own marathon). But at least I could understand what the locals are saying: having been brought up in Sunderland I can 'tak proper' in fluent Geordie. The runners assemble in a park. By now they resemble aliens walking around wrapped in aluminium foil with large bottles of water attached to their faces. We scan the silver sea, but it's like looking for a needle in a haystack. Where's David? At last we see him walking towards us. He's done it! He's raised £1,500 for Leukaemia Research. We phone Jonathan immediately to tell him the good news. Jonathan tries not to be too impressed (it's his kid brother, after all), but happily fails.

YEAR 2000 ARRIVES, THEN 2001

The year 2000 has arrived. Jonathan celebrates the new millennium on the banks of The Thames. The rest of the family also party, each of us in different places with different groups of people, but the first thing we do after the last chime rings out is to call each other to wish 'health, wealth and happiness'.

It's a milestone year for our family. Peter and I celebrate our Silver Wedding Anniversary. After much thought, we decide against a Family and Friends gathering (because God knows we see enough of them) and opt to travel to the USA. I fall in love with New York, like everyone does.

Jonathan graduates from Greenwich University. When the results arrive, he is extremly irate because he's only been awarded a 2:1. He says he'd 'worked out' that he should have got a First. He turns over the slip he reads that his degree is in Nursing and that he did very well in the Midwifery module.

He is on the phone immediately. Questions are asked , issues raised (and yes, tempers flare). Yes, indeed, he should have been awarded a First in Media and Society. The paper work is corrected. The rebel has won his cause. Once again I am left emotionally drained. I would be delighted to pass a degree, but to gain a first after the year he has endured. What a remarkable young man he is! I am the proudest Mum in the world.

The graudation ceremony takes place in Greenwich Maritime College in July. I dress for the occasion in a lilac suit and navy blue hat. I am proud of my appearance and really feel I look the part. I confidently enter the bar where we have arrranged and am greeted by Jonathan with 'What do you look like!?' Now, where many parents would be offended by this, I immediately realise this is Jonathan-speak for 'You look good, Mum.' At the ceremony, when Jonathan is presented with his degree, the other course members cheer loudly.

He begins work at Web Broadcast Media. He shares a flat with friends in London. Life goes on. Hospital visits are just an inconvenience.

We celebrate Jonathan taking the last of the 10, 000 tablets that made up his Chemo on Boxing Day. We all have a champagne toast to the future.

2001 has arrived. The year gets off to a good start. Jonathan has a new job at AOL. He travels to New York with his brother David. They celebrate David's 21st at the top of The Empire State Building.

And then in April Jonathan mentions that he has backache.

From: jon [shoes@clara.co.uk]

Sent: 10 May 2001 19:51

Subject: Update 10/5

So here I am again. As most of you know, I was diagnosed with a relapse of my Acute Lymphoblastic Leukaemia just over two weeks ago. I've begun a programme of chemotherapy which is leading up to a bone marrow transplant some time in June if things go well.

At present I am living at Queen Elizabeth Hospital Woolwich. I'm here because, after finishing my studies in Greenwich, I declined to transfer my care from there. Greenwich Hospital closed down 6 weeks ago, and the staff were transplanted wholesale to this lovely new hospital in Woolwich. Unfortunately, it makes getting to and from my flat in Islington nearly impossible. Public transport is considered too much of a health risk (well, let's face it, that's true for everyone), and when a cab costs the best part of 50 quid you don't want to be making the trip on a daily basis.

I was let out for the first time last Tuesday, but by Wednesday afternoon I was feeling sick and had to return. I envisage from now on I will be spending the vast majority of my time here. That is, of course, until I have my transplant which we believe will be carried out at UCH[29]. The donor will be one of my brothers, either David or Thomas. The first time I was sick they were not considered suitable donors as they have some superfluous material in their bone marrow that I do not. As the chemotherapy was apparently progressing well enough on its own before, this was considered an unnecessary risk. Apparently this is not the case now, as there have been some advances in the conditioning process in the last 2 years, which will enable me to receive their marrow without too much trouble.

In the meantime, I've been working my way through a course of chemotherapy. I had a very rough first week, picked up a bit and am now in reasonable shape apart from a very sore mouth which makes it difficult to swallow, making eating a problem. Worse, despite what you may have seen on the news about Lloyd Grossman spearheading a new improved hospital food campaign, the meals are still for the most part inedible. The vegetarian choice is typically something mouthwatering like cauliflower crumble or cheese and egg custard. Marvellous. I had arranged with the catering staff to receive Asian vegetarian meals and had been enjoying Gobi Aloo Saag and such, but with my mouth all messed up now I'm surviving on soup and yoghurts. The doctors suggest the cocaine mouthwash again. My eyes lit up at the possibility, as this seems like another excellent way to help pass the day.

Speaking of which I have a laptop and, through surreptitious use of my mobile phone, I am able to send and receive emails from my bed.

I think these prolonged periods in hospital surrounded by pensioners is turning me into an old git. When this kind of thing-and having to wait for my newspaper until nearly 11-winds me up I know I'm prematurely ageing. On the subject of pensioners I heard the other day that the train robber Ronnie Biggs may be transferred here if Belmarsh prison's medical facilities prove inadequate. Mind you with the crooked cleaning staff (who, after I left the room for 24 hours, managed to dispose of a box of tissues, an unopened can of diet coke and half a box of sweets that my good friend Celene had brought me from

29 University College Hospital, London.

Florida, despite assurances that they would touch nothing) he should fit right in, and what with all these class A drugs kicking around too...

In general, then, things are progressing as well as could be expected. The doctors here are very good. I've had no trouble in getting answers to my questions, and they visit me regularly. The nurses are generally all really nice too, and like I said, with this being a brand new hospital, the facilities are generally very good. Next week I should start my second course of chemotherapy, so I might be a feeling a bit rough for a while, hopefully not for too long.

Looking forward to seeing you all soon,

Jon

From: jon [shoes@clara.co.uk]

Sent: 17 May 2001 18:43

Subject: Update 17/5

I'm back at home again, hopefully this time for a little longer than 24 hours. Glancing at the clock I see I'm just about to reach that watermark, so I'd best get this brief missive out of the way before my temperature rockets, I start puking or my leg falls off.

Last week was reasonably uneventful. My mouth soon cleared up, and by the weekend I was perfectly able to eat normally. Hospital cuisine remained inedible however, so a mixed blessing really. I did enjoy the treatment though. I heartily recommend cocaine mouthwash to anyone who is admitted to hospital for any reason whatsoever. Unfortunately they are not made available to outpatients, so I have been deprived of a potentially lucrative means of supplementing my meagre income-support payments. I must add that it was only after swallowing 2 or 3 of these treatments that a doctor informed that they were not intended for internal consumption. How was I to know?

Tony Blair visited the hospital at the weekend, but I wasn't allowed to leave the ward and go looking for him. There had quite obviously been some directive issued from the Home Office to make sure that potential troublemakers were confined to their beds.

By Wednesday morning I'd finished the course of IV antibiotics that I'd been prescribed (whilst my mouth was sore I was showing a temperature so they wanted to kill off any potential infection), and my blood counts were looking as well as can be expected. Dr Kettly gave me the all clear to go home and we had a chat about the timetable for my treatment. It looks as if I was a little optimistic with my initial appraisal of how long I might be in hospital. I'm returning to hospital on Monday for a blood test, and if my counts are high enough they'll take a bone marrow sample. That will then be sent over to the professor (who's name escapes me) at UCH, who will be conducting my transplant. Then I'm going to go over and meet said prof in order to discuss my treatment. Then after all of that I'll begin my second course of chemotherapy, which will be end of May / start of June by then.

Assuming course 2 follows the same pattern as course 1, I should be in hospital for the first of half of June and then hopefully well enough to come out in time for Tony and Celene's wedding on the 23rd. That means my bone marrow transplant will not be taking place until July or perhaps even August. I'm a little concerned about this as I don't want to miss the whole summer. I had really hoped to be fit by September, before the lease on my flat runs out and I have to make some tough decisions about what I'm doing with myself. Oh well, just have to take it as it comes, I guess.

Learning to solve cryptic crosswords was one of my plans for passing the time in hospital, but it has run aground already. Dad bought me a book which explained how the clues work, and I felt quite pleased with myself as I progressed from complete novice to tabloid level. Unfortunately the *Guardian* and *Times* crosswords remain utterly incomprehensible. Despite what the book says I remain convinced that you need to be the sort of person who quotes Latin on a daily basis, can give a blow-by-blow account of the Battle of Bosworth Field and can name every member of the England cricket team ever to be able to complete them. My lack of a classical education (I only know the first five letters of the Greek alphabet after all) is painfully evident.

Sod it, can someone buy me a Playstation 2 instead?

Jon

FRACTURE – ARTICLE, MID-MAY 2001

'To have leukaemia once may be seen as unfortunate, to have it twice could be perceived as careless,' to paraphrase Oscar Wilde

As many of you already know I have been diagnosed with a relapse of Acute Lymphoblastic Leukaemia and have been undergoing chemotherapy treatment for a month or so now in the delightful Queen Elizabeth Hospital of Woolwich, London. It's the newest in the country, even being visited by Tony Blair during the election campaign.

I have a fancy electric adjustable bed of the kind you see advertised in-between pensioners' TV shows like *Watercolour Challenge*, and a sort of in-flight entertainment system thing with digital TV, radio and phone. Actually the Patientline 'service', as it's known is a point of contention. I dislike the rather Orwellian manner in which it is impossible to turn the screen off during the daytime, and I object to being woken at 8am every morning with GMTV. The Today programme on Radio 4 would be fine, but I just can't abide morning television. Furthermore the phone line, whilst cheap (compared to a payphone) for me to use is prohibitively expensive to call from outside. 50 pence a minute thank you very much. I figure if they're going to run a premium rate number then I, as the main attraction, should get a cut. They could have ads on Channel 5 with a bunch of patients attached to drips shuffling along to a faux house soundtrack whilst a narrator intones 'call 0898 66 66 66 now for red hot live oncology ward chat.'

I received an email today from UCH Euston, which is where I'll be moving to before long for my bone marrow transplant[30]. It's a lot closer to where I live, and apparently I might be housed in a special 'adolescent' room with a net connected iMac, Limp Bizkit posters for wallpaper, a bed in the shape of a racing car, and taps that spew coca cola instead of water. I made up everything except for the iMac, but that's good enough for me. I do have my laptop with me of course, but at the moment I have to dial up via my mobile phone which is neither cheap nor fun.

---

30 Jonathan was initially told that a transplant would be impossible. Why these conditions changed are explained by him in the next chapter.

I am in touch with the world though, and emails are always appreciated.

By the time you read this I may already be in at UCH. The date of the transplant has been set: Friday July 20th. There's a week of preparation chemo and total body irradiation beforehand, and then a cool six weeks afterwards to recover before I get to go home. The doctor assures me that I will feel quite terrible for a long time and can write off the rest of the year as far as having a 'normal' life is concerned. Well, I appreciate his candour at least.

The youngest of my three younger brothers, Thomas, is to be my bone marrow donor. This is handy because he's just finished his A-levels and will be sat around the house doing nothing, whilst David will be busy learning how to kill people with the Royal Marines and Christopher equally occupied performing wheelspins, burnouts and handbrake turns along with hordes of similarly culturally impaired youngsters in carparks throughout the East Midlands.

I'm confident about the transplant. Of course there are risks, and I have been given a percentage, which I'll keep to myself for now. It's quite chilling to hear your life expressed that way, quantified into survival rates, but I asked, they told me, so that's that[31]. Apparently my case is 'not overly complex' so we're not expecting any troubles beyond the usual litany of complaints: nausea, fatigue, sickness, loss of appetite, vomiting, diarrhoea, alopecia, infertility and so on. The biggest risk is from infections, which my immune system, having been entirely depleted prior to transplant, will be unable to counter. I will be forbidden from eating takeaway food, and this includes pizza. It will be a long, hard and painful recovery.

I always try to take something positive from every aspect of my illness. It gave me the perfect reason to quit my job, despite their offers of sick pay. I didn't like it, and although my employers treated me well, I didn't want to feel indebted to return to them. I've decided to pursue my ideal vocation of

---

31 This is not an estimate of chances of death, as is commonly understood. A patient is given a percentage chance of both surviving the transplant and of the leukaemia never recurring.

writing professionally and will most probably return to university to study for an appropriate MA. When I'm in hospital I have an abundance of time for reading and writing; when out of hospital I can saunter round London like a tourist, enjoying the benefits of our extortionate rents.

Surprising it may sound, but hospital treatment allows for quite wonderful experimentation with class A drugs. With an on demand prescription for diamorphine, genuine cases of pain relief soon turned into flagrant recreational usage. Cocaine mouthwashes, prescribed for soreness, are tremendous fun, especially when you swallow them in front of your parents. So you see, it's not all needles and drips here on the ward. The food however is as disgusting as one would expect, and doubly so for vegetarians like myself (Cauliflower Crumble anyone?).

I write this now on one side of a long dark tunnel. The transplant, its preparation and recovery, will be unpleasant in the extreme. I hope that I can be so upbeat the next time I write.

We've all spent so much time trying to remain positive and yet somehow the leukaemia has returned. Hasn't it been listening?

This time around though, the choice has been easy. I completely forget about work and elect to stay with Jonathan. Who's supporting who is a good question, but it doesn't really matter.

A problem arises as to where I'll stay. The brand new hospital at Woolwich has everything except accommodation for visitors /relatives. We begin a tour of the area. Most places are fully booked; many will not take a woman on her own (in this day and age?). One volunteers to charge me by the hour! I decline; the décor leaves a great deal to be desired. At last a bed is found; a mere snip at £110 per night! But it includes breakfast and is on a bus route to the hospital.

A new routine commences with new names to learn and new surroundings. Remaining positive is the order of the day. Some of the regime is all too familiar: another Hickman Line, lumbar punctures, blood tests, samples of this that and the other, charts to complete. And mood swings.

The staff at Woolwich are wonderful: Dr K with his bright shirts and gaudy braces; Dr Mike, calm, positive, encouraging; Nahm the nurse, French and glamorous. She establishes such a rapport with Jonathan...if only circumstances were different.

The most amazing person of all is Andy, an assistant on the ward. Dedicated to feeding the patients, Andy is a man with a mission. Nothing is too much trouble.

> *'Here we go, mate, nice bit of fish on today.'*
> *'I'm a vegetarian.'*
> *'Well, there's gooo-lash stuff.'*
> *'Ok?'*
> *'Sprouts with it, mate?'*

By the end of the first week Jonathan has exhausted the entire vegetarian repertoire. Much to our dismay each and every meal is accompanied by frozen sprouts. Has the NHS bought a cheap job lot or is it a ploy to ensure regularity?

Then the next bout of chemo kicks in, and food is no longer an issue. With his usual determination, Jonathan informs the doctors that he MUST be finished by the middle of June as he has a friend's wedding to attend.

Time, remarkably, doesn't drag. The days are full. I study, read, make Christmas cards and explore the locality. It's bearable. Money is slipping through my fingers, though. I did finally find a very pleasant B&B at £20 per night, but that's still £140 a week. On top of that there are bus and train fares to pay, lunch, dinner, drinks, snacks, newspapers, phone calls, etc, etc. In addition, if Jonathan wants to watch television, PatientLine has to be paid for. In all, it costs two or three hundred pounds a week to stay with Jonathan.

We both regard it rather like an adventure, a time to be together, a time to get closer. Jonathan, with his high intellect and proud determination, reluctantly comments that he 'kind of likes having Mum around'. Myself, worried sick but pretending not to be, I'm just relieved to be with him. Yet at the same time I'm torn because my husband and other sons were left at home to fend for themselves. I even worry that the cats are not being fed properly. I miss my work, especially the children; I feel that I'm letting them down. I feel guilty, I feel sad, and I feel angry. But, then again, none of these must be anything like what Jonathan is feeling.

Good news comes very quickly. We have the choice of three hospitals that are prepared to offer Jonathan a transplant. Previous experience makes us rather wary, though – it seems too good to be true.

Life at Woolwich is rather mundane. We just aim to get through. Visitors are always much appreciated. Many of them travel over an hour across London to come, and those who are unable to visit called or emailed. Friends of all religions and faiths pray for him.

Which reminds me, one afternoon there is a tentative knock on the door and in comes a lady who announces that she's the Ward Chaplin and has come to lead us in prayer. Jonathan's face says it all. We aren't religious at the worst of times. The last thing we want is religion thrust on us. She made the error, too, of arriving when Neighbours was about to start. NOTHING stops Jonathan from watching Neighbours.

My diversionary tactic is to tell the Chaplin that Jonathan is tired, and that she and I could go and have a chat in the day room. The sacrifices a mother must make. One thing that soon becomes apparent is that she's well informed on Jonathan's medical history. I ask how she knew so much about him. She openly admits that she's read his notes.

I am furious at this! What right has she to read his notes without asking first? She says she needs to know the patient's background. I say that Jonathan does not wish nor ever has wished to have contact with any form of religious support. She insists she has the right to know. If you ask me, I think she's a prying gossip. As a teacher, I'm not allowed access to the children's medical records, and I respect confidentiality. Why doesn't she have to follow the same professional code of conduct?

I must disguise my anger well because she keeps talking. I stop listening, planning a timely escape. It can't come soon enough.

I return to Jonathan's room only to find him not in the best of moods either. He's had a run in with the matriarchal sister over visitors. When Jonathan was in the side ward, he had agreed to keep an eye on elderly Bert for his wife Ivy. In return, Bert would call for the nurses when Jonathan was in pain and needed more morphine. Ivy, being a typical Grandma, had a handbag stuffed full of goodies. Now in his new room, Ivy, concerned for Jonathan, had ventured in, asked how he was, and committed the crime of offering him a banana!

Sister was not pleased; she had actually thrown Ivy out and then proceeded to reprimand Jonathan. Jonathan stood his ground. He liked Ivy because she reminded him of his own Grandma and he wanted to know how Bert was. Surely this was acceptable? Sister was obviously used to being obeyed without question. How dare a patient, and a young one at that, question her? She informed Jonathan that Ivy was now 'barred' from visiting him because of the possibility of infection. Jonathan's retort was to enquire if the Chaplin could visit.

Sister beamed, 'Of course.'

'Well,' he replied, 'I don't want a visit from the Chaplin or any religious type. I'll trade it for a visit from Ivy. I HAVE THE RIGHT TO CHOOSE MY VISITORS!'

'But it's hospital policy for the Chaplin to visit,' stated Sister and hastily left the room.

I like to think of myself as a calm and easy-going person who will always listen to someone's point of view. But this afternoon I feel so angry. No hospital has the right to thrust religion onto a patient, make it easy for non-medical staff to access notes, or veto visitors. I hope Jonathan and I have provided several items to discuss at the next ward meeting! Jonathan is not in hospital for fun. He's going through chemo, a rough ride at the best of times, so why make it more difficult for him?

One thing all of the hospitals have always promoted is making the most of opportunities to get out for short periods. Now and then, we manage a couple of hours at the cinema and consume a cardboard pizza. We visit Greenwich for a Mexican meal and Woolwich for noodles.

Jonathan is allowed to return to his flat for a couple of days. It's a mess. Jonathan is very down hearted, worryingly so. Don't his flatmates realise that everything has to be as clean as possible? Why this? Why that? I put most of this down to apprehension, i.e., is it really o.k. to be so far from the hospital? The closest tube station to his flat was Finsbury Park, the other side of the city from the hospital.

I'm reluctant to leave Jonathan alone, so we reach a compromise whereby I'll stay at the flat until the weekend when his flat mates will be around. We venture out on a short walk to Tesco. Jonathan puts on a brave face, but he's weak and finds it all a bit too much. I begin to worry (well, when do I ever stop?). Passersby look at his gaunt appearance, note the *numerous needle marks on his forearms, draw their own conclusions, avert their eyes, and quickly move on. We make it back to flat and sit down to watch a DVD. Jonathan looks terrible. Despite his protests I fuss. I take his temperature, only to have my fears confirmed: it's too high and we need to return to the hospital. How? It's almost five o'clock, and we have to get across London. We call a mini cab. The driver, bless him, is quick to clock our dilemma. He speeds through the streets taking every possible short cut, but it still takes an hour to reach our destination and costs sixty pounds. At Woolwich, medication is administered and things are back under control.*

Just another 'typical' day! I wonder which is worse: the tedium of being an in- patient or the anxiety of being an out- patient? Not being able to make plans or confirm arrangements becomes a way of life. No matter how many times you say to yourself take it an hour at a time and be thankful for each extra day, it doesn't get any easier.

From: jon [shoes@clara.co.uk]

Sent: 30 May 2001 10:53

Subject: Update 30/5

I've managed to keep myself out of trouble and out of hospital for the last week or two, save for a couple of pre-arranged appointments. The first of which was to have bone marrow sample taken last Thursday. I think the increasingly battered state of my veins is becoming a little too much for Woolwich's nursing staff. One of them fell faint while try-ing to draw blood from me. Surely the wrong way around?

The bone marrow went OK, despite Dr Bagi waking me from my seda-tion to show me a dozen bloody smears held between two panes of glass which he thought I might be interested in. I later learnt that these were my bone marrow results, and they thankfully showed me to be in complete remission again, which is good news.

Went back to Grantham for the weekend, forgot completely how my tolerance for alcohol had been affected, paid for my oversight quite harshly on Sunday night. Took the train back to London on Tuesday morning, so I could make my appointment with the Professor at UCH Euston. That Eric Burks character (at least I think that's his name) was there, you know the 'monster monster' cigar chomping sports agent and pundit type guy. My meeting with the Prof went OK, considering. Up until then I'd been quite upbeat about things, but I left quite despondent after being given the low-down on just how traumatic the transplant process is going to be. He also told me that I could pretty much write off the rest of this year. I guess I knew this anyway. I'm always overly optimistic as to the predicted duration of my treatment.

Of some small consolation was the news that they have four rooms for adolescent patients at UCH, and though I'm supposedly a grown up patient who shouldn't require such comforts, they may be able to make one available to me, complete with iMac and internet connection. My transplant should be around the middle of July, though they still have to do a couple more tests to decide which of my brothers to use.

After hospital Mum and I went down to the South Bank so we could go on the London Eye (for my American friends, it's the giant Ferris Wheel across the river from Big Ben). Mum doesn't like heights and required some cajoling, but I was far more worried about the prospect of being trapped in a glass capsule for half an hour with a whole class of screaming French school children. The view from the Eye is magnificent, and it was a beautiful day, though the strong sunlight made the capsules very hot. I must have been feeling masochistic as I then suggested we walk up to Covent Garden so we could endure hordes of German tourists gawping in amazement at the inexplicably popular non-singing, non-dancing, non-doing-anything-at-all human statues. I bought some new trainers which will come in handy for sitting around in hospital (when I go back to Woolwich on Friday for a second batch of chemotherapy), and then got sunburnt.

Jon

Yet another hospital.

Our first impressions of UCH are not ideal. It's a hot sticky day. Emotions are throbbing a bit. We arrive at reception only to be told that we're in the wrong place. The building resembles a dilapidated rabbit warren with everyone going round in circles. Phones ringing, buzzers buzzing, the whole place looks unkempt and uncared for.

I can sense the anger rising in Jonathan. Oh, hell, I think, he's going to snap and walk out of here! We wait, the chairs are uncomfortable, the magazines tattered and out of date. I flick through the millionth waiting room glossy I've seen in the last two years – words tumbling on the page, my brain not taking in a single one. The waiting is always nerve racking.

Jonathan spots a celebrity at the desk. He assures me I should know the name. I don't.

We are finally led to Mr M the consultant's office. As we enter the room, Jonathan and Mr M make eye contact. The air is electric. I can only describe it as a clash of personalities! They glare at each other: words are few, monosyllabic and tinged with a terse directness that sets your teeth on edge. Mr M comes straight to the point. Yes, a transplant will take place from either David or Thomas (Christopher was not a match, being a different blood group). The transplant will be most unpleasant and cannot be guaranteed a success, nor can it be repeated. It's up to Jonathan whether he wants to go through with it.

At the first opportunity Jonathan storms out – swearing. Foul words fill the air, spat out at anyone who might be listening. I feel quite sick, the realities of the situation hitting home. Again. But in his way Jonathan is asking for my help and support. He has a decision to make.

His first reaction is to refuse the transplant. I allow him to rant and rave and expend his frustrations. I wait for him to calm down. My proud/arrogant /intelligent/strong- willed son will need to be reasoned with eventually.

I suggest a drink. We go to a pub. The lunchtime drinkers don't give us a thought. Why should they? After all they have their own decisions to make: is there enough time for another half before returning to work?

How can life be so bloody cruel? Why my son? Why? I want to scream out loud but I have to stay calm enough to persuade Jonathan to consider the transplant.

As I walk to the bar to order the drinks I take a deep breath. I tell myself to smile, be positive. Again. Tears well up in my eyes. Again. I collect the drinks and walk back to the table. Jonathan is staring at the floor. His fists are clenched; he's leaning forward. His body language is conveying the message 'leave me alone'. I resist the urge to wrap my arms around him and kiss him better. Instead I sit quietly and wait. And wait and wait. At last he raises his eyes and looks at me. I can see the fear reflected in them. He's weak and vulnerable.

'Ready to talk, Son?' I ask as calmly as I can.

'Why should I bother? To go through all of that, and then it might not even work,' he snaps.

'It's a Hobson's Choice. If you don't try, you'll always wonder what if. Two years ago you were devastated when you were refused a transplant. Now medical science has advanced enough to provide you with the opportunity to take a chance, have a go. What have you got to lose?"

Silence

'But he's (Mr M) such an arrogant bastard.'

'Yes, love he's a lot like you. Tells it how it is, doesn't make false promises. Isn't it better we're told from the start that it may not work? Dr M is a very clever man and all that, an expert in his field and so on, but perhaps his people skills are a little lacking. Come on son is there really an easy way to tell a stranger what he has had to tell you?'

Jonathan agrees he'll go ahead with the transplant.

I cry. It's relief and fear.

※   ※   ※

Our return visit to UCH follows much the same lines as before. We are stuck in the car for hours just to keep yet another hospital appointment. David and Thomas are with us, as potential bone marrow donors. Three six foot plus males and myself wedged into a Ford Fiesta. Why didn't we take the train? Tempers are fraught as we negotiate the one-way traffic system. At last a parking space, a mere snip at £4 an hour. It's a relief to stretch our legs.

We meet Jonathan, so that makes five of us cluttering up the waiting room. The same old magazines lay strewn across the tables and chairs. Jonathan slumps into a chair. I thrust The Guardian *towards him. 'See if you can beat Dad and finish the crossword first.'*

Jo the transplant nurse/coordinator and Dr Emma arrive. More tests are needed. Another obstacle to overcome: GVH[32]. Also checks to ensure that both David and Thomas are certain what donating bone marrow will entail. Have they realised that it may cause them pain and discomfort? Has the family pressurised them into being donors? They're taken in turn to another room to discuss this. Peter misreads the situation and insists on accompanying the boys I give him one of my special 'sit down and behave' looks but it fails to register.

Jonathan is by now engrossed in the crossword. I leave him be. Close my eyes and pray.

Jo returns with an update, which we already knew: both boys were willing to donate bone marrow, they still could be deemed unsuitable. Yet another waiting game.

We had been previously told that Jonathan's type of bone marrow was quite rare, but that genetically his make up was most like mine. This had been established via a set of blood tests. Getting blood from me is not an easy process. The lab technician entered the back of my hand for attempt number seven, and I began to feel very sick. The room was spinning. Jonathan was so concerned. 'Just leave it, Mum,' he said. I looked up. There were tears in his eyes. How could I give up? We could never give up. There had to be hope, always.

My mind is focussing on the reality that a bone marrow transplant may not happen. If his brothers did not prove to be suitable, where or when would we find another match? Or worst of all would it come too late?

We all gather to leave. The lifts are busy and we take the stairs. On the way down, the large works of art on the walls fascinate us. Various every day hospital items have been beautifully arranged and photographed. Our favourite is a collection of paper machine urine bottles. As I look at the picture I can't help thinking what wonderful maracas they would make for the children in my Nursery class.

After being inside the gloomy rabbit warren of the hospital, it is a relief to emerge into the bright sunshine and cross the road to the Rosenheim building.

---

32 Graft Versus Host Disease. This is complication whereby the donated cells from Jonathan's brother may begin to attack Jonathan's body rather than helping it.

From: Jon Kay [shoes@clara.co.uk]

Sent: 15 June 2001 17:46

Subject: Update 15/6

'Be here at ten. It's very important that you be here at ten so that we can get your blood counts before the ward round.'

So I brave the London rush hour, all the way from lovely N7 to horrid SE666, and get there as instructed for ten.

I get my blood count results at 4.45pm. They didn't even have a room for me until three.

On my way here I had to endure one bus driver who would neither change a ten pound note nor accept fifty pence in silver (the fare is 70p), followed by a second who couldn't even give change from a pound coin (I let him keep it). I made it in the end though, and my counts are pretty darn low. I'm having some blood and platelets over the weekend, and I'm hoping to get out of here by the middle of next week, in time for Tony and Celene's wedding next Saturday.

To bring you all up to speed: I had some chemotherapy last week and was out of hospital waiting for my counts to drop. They did, and I'm back in now until they pick up. In the meantime I've been enjoying London in the company of two American friends, playing the role of tour guide. This is great because it allows you to do all those things that as a London snob you proclaim 'only for the tourists' but actually wouldn't mind doing yourself. However, this does not include Madame Tusseauds, eating at Aberdeen Steak Houses, or anything involving the words Andrew, Lloyd and Webber. I still have my standards.

UCH have been in contact via email. I have a schedule for my bone marrow transplant. The conditioning will begin on the 13th of July with chemotherapy and full body irradiation for seven days[33], then on Friday the 20th the transplant itself. There's a week of follow-up treatment and then the recovery which could mean me staying in for another month or so. Thomas has been selected as the most favoured

---

33 Actual treatment is two doses of chemotherapy a day for three days.

choice of donor. This was due to him being both the same blood group and CMV negative like me (a harmless virus that half the population has, it helps if donor and recipient match, regardless of whether positive or negative). Everything seems to be progressing well on the transplant front. I'll have more details when I go over there for some consultation visits in a couple of weeks.

Otherwise not much else going on really. I lost £10 in a bet on the election. I had the Lib Dems at 5-1 to win between 53 and 56 seats. They got 52. I blame the Isle of Wight, though if they want to be Tory scum than that's their choice I suppose. Not that I'm bitter or anything. I was going to have a bet on the leadership race, but Portillo looks like a cert and the odds reflect that...

I think online politics gambling may be a bad idea for someone on meagre state benefits, especially when I don't actually have any yet. The DSS have done everything in their power to make my illness as uncomfortable as possible. 5 weeks on from first contact and still no money. Plenty of forms to fill out though, non functioning phone numbers to call, and non-existent addresses to visit... I could go on but I really don't have the strength.

Jon

Things don't get any better. We are asked to visit PPW3 in order to meet the staff and familiarise ourselves with the surroundings. Private Patient's Ward Three is in reality a NHS ward situated in the Rosenheim building. The building itself is a relic from a bygone age; the foyer feels distinctly Art Deco, with even some of the original features remain. It almost seems we're moving up market. I wonder if the reading matter in the waiting areas will be of better quality. Doubt it.

As we emerge from the lift, we are immediately confused to find ourselves in the fertility clinic. Peter and I are greeted with a warm welcoming smile from the lady behind the desk. She moves forward, obviously considering us potential clients. She is curtailed by Peter asking for directions to PPW3. The boys find this quite amusing.

Our party ventures through the swing doors and finds itself in a large airy corridor, which for some strange reason is painted with huge blue swirls to represent the sea. We locate the reception desk and state our business.

Everyone is 'busy'. We are asked to wait in the day room.

Wimbledon is on. The room is crowded. We struggle to get a seat, it's very hot, and no one offers us a drink. Our spirits fall. I can sense anger in Jonathan again. The scene is exactly like Nottingham – and boy how he hated that place! We try to cheer him up by drawing his attention to the PC in the corner and the fact that the ward is made up of individual rooms.

At last someone arrives. I don't remember most of what they said. Only two things come out of the conversation. The first, that I could stay in the hospital. The second, that Jonathan may be 'too old' for that ward because it's considered a young persons ward. His 23rd birthday is at the end of the month.

It's suggested that he could end up on PPW2.

As we travel home Jonathan is not best pleased. To him it's been another waste of a day. Yet again he's spent it 'in hospital'.

From: Jon Kay [shoes@clara.co.uk]

Sent: 15 July 2001 00:10

Subject: Update 14/7

Hello all. It's been a while since I last wrote, which is a good thing because it means I've been, for the most part, out of hospital and enjoying myself in between courses of treatment. I finished all my business at Woolwich and moved on to UCH at Euston. It has not been an entirely pleasant transition. Although I moaned about the distance, poor transport links, and a neighbourhood that resembles Beirut rather London, at least at Woolwich I had a brand new shiny and clean room, with en suite of course. I guess it has something to do with the property market. There's a lot more demand here in Zone 1, just off Tottenham Court Road.

I made it quite clear to the staff that I was a very private person and that I liked my own space. They kindly said that they would endeavour to provide me with a single room, even when I'm not immuno-compromised. Well that's happened in a sense... I'm sitting alone in the day care room, which has four beds on one side of the room – each with its own TV so that I can watch four channels simultaneously. There's a big seated area and a water cooler, which is nice, and best of all there's the receptionist's desk where I can make use of a phone point to get online. Unfortunately they're going to kick me out of here tomorrow and send me to a real room because they need it for day patients, obviously.

So I came in to UCH last Friday for a bone marrow harvest. It's essentially the same process my brother will go through when he donates his marrow. My own harvest is a back up in case there are any serious complications when I receive his. It was done under general anaesthetic, which is just as well as I was left with three bullet holes in my back (OK, they're weren't that big, but I swear they were big enough to see in to). I was warned it would hurt, and the anaesthetist mentioned that he could, whilst I was under, insert a suppository painkiller. As tempting as that sounded, I declined, being the long term strategist that I am. The logic of this is that if I woke up in pain I could ask for a stronger painkiller. And that would be diamorphine. The hours would just fly by. Unfortunately it appears that UCH do not share Woolwich's enlightened stance of prescribing class A drugs to its patients. Diamorphine requires repeated insistence. Cocaine mouthwash is not on the menu. Damn.

I returned home after the bone marrow harvest before returning on Monday night to have my Hickman line fitted first thing on Tuesday morning. Another procedure under general anaesthetic, and here's an interesting thing – when in hospital one has to wear a name band around the wrist. When going into the operating theatre a second and completely identical band must be worn around the opposite wrist. I asked why this was necessary, but no-one appeared to know. I suggested that it may be to ensure that, should my chart get mixed up with the arm amputation they have to do later, there will still be one tag left on me. I was told that, on the haematology ward, they don't really get to do many arm amputations.

That said, I was having a cigarette (I know, I know) in the smoking room (yes!) with a maudlin fellow from Liverpool who was having his gangrenous toes amputated as a result of the dodgy smack he'd shot into his thighs. A nasty business. I could go on here on why I believe 'clean' heroin (i.e. diamorphine) should be prescribed to addicts, and why I believe that in the case of drugs, the law is an ass, but I've run on for long enough already. Another time perhaps.

After the Hickmann line was fitted I went home for a couple of days, had a lovely 'last supper' at La Porchetta, the finest pizzeria in North London, and after spending Friday being fucked around by income support, then the hospital, then housing benefit, then the hospital again, I finally started my chemotherapy this morning. As a taste of things to come, it went OK, I suppose. It made me feel sick after only 20 minutes of a two hour bag.

Fortunately, the anti-sickness tablets they have here seem to work very well, and an hour or so after it was finished I was well enough to eat. The food here is as bad, if not worse than that at Woolwich, but as we are surrounded by takeaways and restaurants, my Mum has been providing an excellent delivery service. More of the same tomorrow (Sunday), and then Monday, Tuesday and Wednesday I have 2 doses of full body irradiation each day. Hair loss is one thing, and sterility is a bummer, but I really hope it doesn't damage my tattoo. Thursday chemo for me whilst my brother Thomas gets the 'harvester' treatment. I should warn him about the suppository. And the arm amputations, of course. Then Friday 20th of July I get new bone marrow! I think in years to come, should it prove successful, I'll celebrate it as a kind of second birthday, like the Queen does.

Jon

Jonathan is allocated a bed on PPW2. I am allocated a much-appreciated relative's room 'out the back'.

There is something warm and comforting about the ward. Yes, at first glance it was like stepping back in time and things were rather frayed around the edges. But what really makes the difference is the staff. There is an air of total competence about the place, an unrivalled professionalism.

We are greeted with a cheery hello and a welcoming smile. Yes, we are expected, they know who we are and what we're here for. A nice change. A cup of tea is provided while we wait in the day room. The nursing staff are young and vibrant. Much to my relief there appear to be a large proportion of males on staff. (Jonathan has always responded better to male nurses. Females tended to fall into the following categories: additional Mother figures, battle axes, waste of space or if-I-weren't-in-here-I'd-ask-her-out.) Male staff are just that- staff. There isn't the same embarrassment in discussing bowel movements and the like with a fellow male.

Jonathan is placed in a side day ward at first. He wants his own room. It takes a great deal of tact and diplomacy on my part to remind him that we were not in a hotel. He says he won't go through with the treatment unless he's in an individual room. He demands his privacy. Things calm down a little and he begins to read the Guardian.

Now, any self-respecting female knows that you do not come between a man and his newspaper. In hospital, however, things are a bit different. A nurse arrives and plonks herself down on Jonathan's bed. Big mistake number one: she's invaded his space! Big mistake number two: she begins to go through his details, name, address, age and the like. He barely acknowledges her because he's engrossed in one of the articles in the paper. Things are not going well. Undaunted, the nurse plods on. Sensing Jonathan's irritation, I offer my assistance. It's rejected. Then the nurse made the biggest mistake of all: she begins to explain Jonathan's treatment to him in the simplest of terms. He's seething by this time. She mentions a drug pronouncing the name slowly and carefully.

Jonathan flings down the paper, instantly earning the Most Difficult Patient of the Week Award in the process. 'Had that before, but the dosage was changed to x because of side effects. We also talked about using y, but agreed on x. I expect to discuss my treatment with medical staff.'

Oh, hell, I thought, we've only been here a couple of hours. He's like a bear with a sore head. Where's the chocolate? Boy, could I eat a bar right now.

The next morning Jonathan is moved to his own room. The more experienced staff is assigned to administer to him. Obviously he's already acquired the reputation of a demanding patient who has to have his mother with him to keep him under control.

From: Jon Kay [shoes@clara.co.uk]

Sent: 30 July 2001 15:11

Subject: update 30/7

Two weeks since I last wrote, and what a fortnight it's been! It seems I've been in UCH forever. I finally made it into a room of my own, and without having to spend any time in a shared room! Thankfully I have a huge room now with TV and video, electric adjustable bed, phone, but no en suite. Shame. Unfortunately, I'm only able to make 0800 calls from my phone, so I have to use my mobile for internet and so on. The nurses are very understanding, however, and let me use their office and computers when I'm well enough to go outside.

I began my first week here with radiotherapy. Not much fun. Twice each day, Mum and I walk ten minutes to the Middlesex Hospital and then wait at least half an hour for our appointment which we had arrived on time for. Radiotherapy involves lying on one's back with a wooden wedge under the knees. Radiotherapy tables are not designed for anyone over five foot six. Your body is packed in with heavy bags of gel to minimise movement and to present a uniform profile to the machine. On the ceiling are two 'spot the difference' pictures for children, which have not been changed since 1984. As each session takes half an hour, the novelty wears off very quickly. The staff are thoughtful enough to allow patients to bring their own music to play on the theatre stereo. As the machine buzzes, the orderlies-pop-tarts to a man (and woman) -sneak off to the reception area and take the piss out of your choices (Mum told me).

There is no immediate sickness from TBI (Total Body Irradiation), unlike the cranial radiotherapy I had the first time round. A few hours after treatment I find myself vomiting, and after a few days tiredness and reddened skin. After my third day of TBI, and sixth session, I was glad to see the end of it. Uncomfortable and tiresome for sure, made worse by a combination of poor weather and an incompetent transport service between the two hospitals.

On Thursday my schedule moved on to chemotherapy, which again had little immediate effect. That evening Thomas and Dad came down in order to check in Tom for the next day's transplant. On Friday morning Tom went into theatre whilst I had some more chemo. A few hours later Jo, the transplant co-coordinator, came into my room brandishing a huge bag of red slop. This was Tom's bone marrow, soon to become mine. After some checks and tests it was hooked up to my Hickman line and my body just sucked it in. The 'transplant' itself is quite an anti-climax, much the same as receiving blood. As for Tom, he woke up woozy from the anaesthetic and kept throwing up the rest of the day. 'Welcome to my life,' I told him. He was OK in the end. I think he even got over the trauma of receiving a suppository painkiller. The next day he went home, and I continued with my chemotherapy.

This is the tough part of the process. After the radiotherapy you have no bone marrow, and with the chemo, no immune system. The donor marrow can take around three weeks to 'graft' so the interim period is uncomfortable and dangerous. Last week I suffered from terrible, terrible stomach cramps, so bad I had to have the nurses knock me out with painkillers. My mouth has become progressively sore, and eating solids almost impossible as my body cannot replace the fast growing cells that line the interior of my mouth and throat. To numb the pain I went from mild mouthwashes, to occasional diamorphine injections and now a constant diamorphine infusion. The diamorphine pump has a patient control which allows me to infuse myself with an extra 5ml of diamorphine when required. Unfortunately this is limited to once an hour at present, so I have not been able to engage in any, ahem, research.

Like all good leukaemia patients, I have now lost all the hair from my head. My eyebrows are thinning out too. I've been vomiting a fantastic range of colours and consistencies, and needless to say I'm constantly exhausted. Hospital is a place where you fall asleep, only to be woken by a nurse and told, 'you should get some rest now.' Indeed.

I've been doing quite well the last few days. I had a tube inserted in my nose and down into my stomach in order to feed me, as the doctors were worried about me not eating enough. Aside from being an extremely painful procedure and an uncomfortable sensation once fitted, it didn't actually work and was removed after an hour or so. I have so far managed to avoid a repeat fitting by consuming plenty of high-fat milkshakes, ice creams and soups. I really hope they don't try and fit another. The docs are also slightly concerned about my Hickmann line not sitting quite right, so they're talking about a temporary line in my neck. I'm doing everything I can to avoid either of these eventualities.

Keep your fingers crossed for me.

Jon

The days on PPW2 fall into a pattern:

After another restless night, I am woken by the noise of the staff wishing each other good morning as they change in the adjacent room.

The day begins with a quick visit to the loo. I know the routine by heart:

open alcohol swab, wipe door handle, taps, loo handle then loo seat. Some days this is done in a bit of rush if I'm desperate to use the toilet or if I have had to wait. It's a must on EVERY visit. After using the facilities a thorough hand washing is also a must.

Off to the shower. Get dressed. Enter ward.

Everyone I meet knows who I am. I feel part of a team- the team caring for Jonathan. We're all on first name terms. Strong bonds have been established. I am given a quick update on the kind of night Jonathan has had.

I knock gently on the door of Jonathan's room. Good, he's asleep. I venture out to buy a newspaper. Although Jonathan is in room one he has questioned hospital procedure by asking WHY he has to be woken for his bloods to be taken. He is first on the ward round. There is no particular reason for this. The ever-considerate staff agree that they will not disturb Jonathan unless absolutely necessary and that he will be last on the ward round.

9.30am the kitchen is open. I make myself some toast and coffee and eat it in the day room watching TV.

I take Jonathan a cup of tea and the newspaper. Usually the doctors have done the ward round by now. Tact and diplomacy is called for. I want to know how he is and what is happening. Questions have to be phrased carefully, moods assessed, the correct moment chosen. If the doctors arrive and I am there, I always respect Jonathan's privacy and ask him if I can stay. The doctors and nursing staff are wonderful discussing medication in detail and involving Jonathan in any decisions to be made.

The doctors seem to thrive on the challenges that Jonathan presents. It's like a battle of great minds. He questions everything, has suggestions to put forward and comments on the quality of his care. The nurses are taken aback by this at first and amazed by the extensive vocabulary Jonathan uses. Despite his strong and demanding personality, I can sense the staff warming to him. I can also sense him warming to the staff. This in turn gives me a sense of security.

Time for a mid morning drink. I settle down to the distance learning college course that I am studying. I need to keep my mind occupied. It's the only way to remain in control and keep the tears at bay. I often wonder how Jonathan does it. Where does the strength come from? He never com-

plains, just gets on with the treatment. The pain must be horrendous, but he remains so positive. I have to stay strong, too.

Some days are better than others. I can tell how Jonathan is by how long he takes to read the paper and do the crossword. The longer he spends the better day he's having.

Interruptions are constant. There's the room to be cleaned. Beds to be made. Blood needs to be taken. Drips put up, taken down, put up again. Hickmanm lines need to be flushed. Phone calls to answer. Bottles to fetch, fluids to measure. And, of course, being sick. Considering he hardly eats a thing, Jonathan has produced amazing quantities of vomit in almost every colour of the rainbow. Sick bowls are continually placed on the bedside table and constantly filled. I buzz for the nurse when things get too bad. Support is always at hand. Anti-sickness tactics are discussed. The most effective medication costs £60 per tablet. Thank goodness these aren't rationed.

Around noon I venture out again in the quest for something for lunch. I find breaking up the day helps me to stay positive. The hospital does of course provide food, but for us the meal times are very early. Also Jonathan has a 'selective' palate. Plus he's vegetarian. It's quite a challenge and expense to provide him with something that will tempt him to eat.

I return yet again to the ward. Things are much the same as before. We watch Neighbours together. Change-over time. The nurses discuss Jonathan's care. He will not participate in the conversation until the pro-gramme has finished. I need to decide how to spend the afternoon. A visit to the shops? A walk? An afternoon nap? The usual choice is a nap. Whatever I decide Jonathan likes to know where I am and what time I expect to return. It's the little things that make you feel valued.

I usually return to his room at 4 o'clock with yet another cup of tea for him and a coffee for me. On a good day he manages a bite of biscuit or cake. On a bad day he throws it straight back up. We watch Countdown and The Weakest Link, scoring points off each other.

While Jonathan watches the six o'clock news, I venture off yet again to select something for dinner. The microwave and toaster in the kitchen are well-used by all. For some strange reason only the nursing staff seem to consume the hospital food. Perhaps it's some part of the training. We usu-ally eat dinner just after seven. Perhaps I should rephrase that. I eat my meal accompanied by a couple of glasses of wine. If Jonathan manages one or two mouthfuls it's a success.

I am a fan of the soaps, and I use this as an excuse to give Jonathan some privacy whilst he contacts his friends. Many come to visit him. These visits are much appreciated. They keep him going, pass the time.

It's now about 10.30pm. I return to Jonathan's room with yet another drink for us both. We may read, listen to music or watch Newsnight. Unlike most of the patients, Jonathan stays up late. At first the staff found this rather unusual. But many use it as an opportunity to chat with him. They are always interested in his diary.

I kiss him goodnight and return to my room. I cry myself to sleep. Another restless night lies ahead. How many more days will we have together? And why should I have to ask myself that question every night?

Transplant Day, July 20th 2001. As Peter sits engrossed in The Guardian, my mind drifts back to Tony and Celene's Wedding the previous month. Jonathan had looked so well as he held court with his many friends. He drank, talked, laughed and danced the night away. Unless you knew, you would never have even guessed he was so ill. That's what is so cruel about Leukaemia; the lack of a large bandage, stitches and a mobility aid make it difficult for outsiders to comprehend the severity of the illness.

Waiting for the transplant is rather like preparing for Christmas: all that hustle and bustle then on the actual day all there is to do is to eat, drink and watch the telly!

Jonathan has been through hell in order to prepare for this. Extensive chemo and radiotherapy, huge amounts of drugs and agonising pain. Morphine's been administered in copious quantities. He's been sick a record-breaking amount of times. At one point he gained an award for projecting vomit the furthest distance when he threw up in the main corridor of PPW2. It took two nurses and myself to clear it up! Sometimes, Jonathan had looked like shit, must have felt like shit, and was sat in shit. Yet he still never moans or complains, just keeps on going with focused determination to get through it all. Above all, he remains totally optimistic that the transplant will be a success.

All I can do was to be there. It breaks my heart to watch him enduring so much pain, but yet again we all have to remain positive.

Thomas has been admitted to PPW3. Time drags, so I wander upstairs to PPW3 to see how he's getting on. It's early, and I wonder if Thomas will even be awake. I enter the room to find a blear- eyed Thomas sitting on the edge of the bed dressed in a hospital gown. I attempt a cheery, rousing conversation but even at the best of times Thomas is a man of few words. He assures me he has no qualms about being a donor. Right now, he seems more pre-occupied with ensuring that the back of his gown does not come open and reveal his posterior.

The trolley arrives. Thomas hesitantly climbs on grasping the gown making certain nothing is on view.

Quick as that, the operation is done. Jo the transplant co-ordinator takes the big red bag of bone marrow from Thomas and then leak it into Jonathan.

Thomas returns from theatre and for the first couple of hours is fine. Then he tries to get out of bed and faints. Then he begins to throw up at frequent intervals. I spend the next few hours climbing up and down the stairs between the two wards, back and forth between two sick boys. Funny how this turns into a way of coping.

We have to wait for a hundred days to learn whether or not the transplant's worked.

From: Jon Kay [shoes@clara.co.uk]

Sent: 15 August 2001 15:30

Subject: Update 15/8

Hello again. Just over three weeks now since I received my brother's bone marrow, and things are running according to schedule.

Here's the big news – my counts started climbing on Saturday. My white blood cell count, which had remained at 0.1 since my chemotherapy began, has now reached the dizzying level of 4.3 (3.4 neutraphils to boot). To put it in layman's terms, I've gone from having no immune system to speak of whatsoever to having reached the low end of an average person's scores (about 4 -1 white blood cells). Most importantly this means that my brother's bone marrow is grafting and that the transplant has been a success so far.

So this is all good and cause for celebration. It's about time too. Last week I was getting increasingly desperate that my counts show some signs of improvement as day after day the came back unchanged. I've already had one treatment regimen fail me, so I did succumb to a certain pessimism at times. Everyone here has been incredibly encouraging however, and at no time did they ever express any doubts about me staging a full recovery.

So here's the thing. Why do I feel so bad? I've been promised since the side effects of the chemotherapy began-the sore mouth, the digestive problems, the exhaustion-that these would all clear up as my counts improved, and I would feel much better, very, very quickly. Well the mouth is a lot more comfortable, it's true, but I've recently been enduring constantly aching heavy limbs, induced by water retention at my joints. I've been sleeping all day and doing anything but at night as I am constantly woken by either the medical staff changing various drips and medications, or by an unbearably painful and frequent urinary tract infection.

Today, though, I'm feeling a little better then before, hence the email. Apologies for the general lack of communication recently by the way. I just haven't had the strength. I did manage to pluck up the strength to get back on the exercise bike this morning, but only for a nice brisk turn down an imaginary country lane. No hill climbs yet. It's also been suggested that I GO OUTSIDE for a while this afternoon. I'm not sure. I know I really should, but I just don't feel like I'm up to it yet. I'm still very unsteady on my feet. Maybe if I had a cane, which I could also use to poke foreign schoolchildren then things perhaps be different.

Despite my improved condition, I am seriously shaky. Although my mouth has cleared up, I'm still not really back on to solid foods yet (I managed a sliver of cheese today). I mainly get by on these hospital made build-up ice cream milk shake things, which are nice but limited to only three flavours. Also, stuff like yoghurts, mousses, etc. Not that I have much appetite. I find myself really wanting to want some pizza, but just not being able to summon up the right feelings. Worrying. I must only be getting a few hundred calories a day in my diet, and it's left me shaky and easily tired. To be honest, I can't see a real return to health until I'm allowed to drink beer again.

More of the same now then. Each day should get a little easier, and by the time I next write I should hopefully be about to leave the hospital. No idea when my hair will grow back though.

Jon

From: Jon Kay [shoes@clara.co.uk]

Sent: 29 August 2001 23:04

Subject: Update 29/8

Hello one and all. This is probably to be the last of my updates, as I'm now out of the hospital and enduring the mundanity of outpatient care, rather than the thrill a minute existence that is ward life. My medication now consists of but twelve tablets a day, six of which admittedly are larger than suppositories and smell like they should be treated as such, and that's about it. I've even had my Hickmann line removed, which is a good thing as it was practically falling out by the time I got to hospital yesterday. I'm glad to be rid of the thing, but now I have no excuse whatsoever for not showering properly. Just because I'm effectively confined to my parents' house doesn't mean I should let my standards slip. In case anyone's interested I'm still completely bald and desperately underweight. I'm eating more and more but I managed to lose another couple of kilos. I need fattening up, please send cakes.

I'll be back down to London on a weekly basis for checkups. I had contemplated transferring my care to Nottingham, but from Grantham (where I am now) it's just as easy to get the train to Kings Cross and then walk or tube it to UCH as it is to drive cross country to Nottingham and then fight for a parking space at City Hospital. Besides I spent some time there the first time I had the big L and despite Professor Russell's reputation as a first rate transplant specialist, I found him to be an arrogant tosser. So UCH it is. Those of you in the big smoke keep an eye out, I'll be around for a while yet.

The rest of this year I'll be in Grantham for the most part, with those occasional sojourns in London and elsewhere. Long term plans include an MA in Journalism next February, which will mean moving to Leeds. I'm hoping to go abroad at the end of this year as a reward to myself, either to see friends in San Francisco or to stay with friends in Hong Kong. In the short term, I'll just be trying to rebuild my strength and keep myself occupied. I've got to watch out for something nasty called Graft versus Host disease. This is the biggy. It's basically a reaction my body might have to its new immune system and can be quite unpleasant. It's most likely within the first 100 days after transplant (we are currently at about 39ish by my reckoning, seen as transplant day was July 20th), but it can occur even after 6 months, which would fuck things up nicely.

So that's it for the time being. I'll be launching my personal portfolio website thing soon, as something to do. I'll send out the address when it goes live. Terribly pretentious and egotistical I know, but gimme a break, I'm living in Grantham for the next 6 months.

Jon

From: Jon Kay [shoes@clara.co.uk]

Sent: 05 September 2001 00:32

Subject: go on, indulge me

Thanks to you all for reading my treatment updates. As I said before I'm not going to be sending them out any more. I'm living at my parents' house now, but still being treated as an outpatient at UCH. At my last checkup (this Monday just past) I was described as a 'model patient', so everything's going as well as can be expected. If there's anything new to report it will find its way to my new website, which is a kind of portfolio type thing. It's located at www.jkay.net. Check it out if you have five minutes to spare.

Thanks,

Jon

SEPTEMBER 2001

The lease has expired on Jonathan's London flat, and he's had to move out. We collect his belongings and return to Grantham. It's a relief to have the entire family under one roof. It's been some months since we all lived together. I still appear to be the only person in our household capable of changing the toilet roll.

At the beginning of September I return to full time work. The school is only a mile or so away from home, but even at this close distance Jonathan's welfare remains my primary concern. Once more I'm torn between family and work responsibilities. Is it always going to be like this?

During the lead up to the transplant, Jonathan decided he would apply to take an M.A. in journalism. He researched various courses on the net and found one that will commence in February 2002. He's asked to come in for a written test. It goes well, and he's optimistic. He has a goal, something to strive for, a new aim.

Then comes the final interview, just a few questions before the few remaining places are allocated.

> *'What have you been doing in recent months? Have you gained any experience working on local newspapers?'*

Jonathan explains his circumstances. A member of the panel fears that his medical condition will mean he is unable to meet the demands of the course. The offer of a place is withdrawn. Jonathan is totally and utterly gutted. His dream has shattered into a million pieces.

Pieces that I have to put together. I suggest he puts it all behind him, seek out another course, remind him that to many people the word CANCER evokes fear, a fear of the unknown, a kind of illness, perhaps that's the reason behind the rejection of his application. He calms down a little but the tears of frustration still well up in his eyes. I pretend not to notice. If I vent my own emotions I will most certainly end up telephoning the admissions panel to give them a piece of my mind. They have rejected my son because they feel that he cannot meet the demands of their poxy little course!! What the hell do they think that Chemo involves – a trip to the seaside?!

Jonathan writes to several local papers and is offered various work placements during the coming months. All is not lost.

On 17th October he sends an email:

'My hospital visit was reassuringly mundane. I don't know if you saw

Living with Cancer on BBC1 on Monday night, but my consultant Dr Steve McKinnon and the ward I was treated on were featured, as well as the radiotherapy department which zapped me twice a day.'

From: Jon Kay [shoes@clara.co.uk]

Sent: 31 October 2001 10:03

Subject: bad news

I just got a call from one of the doctors at UCH. My bone marrow test results have come through, and they're not good. It looks as if my leukaemia has returned. The transplant has been a failure. I'm going down to the hospital with my Dad this afternoon to 'discuss my options.'

I'll let you know more as I find out.

I'm pretty scared.

Jon

From: Jon Kay [shoes@clara.co.uk]

Sent: 01 November 2001 02:59

Subject: bad news in full

I'm sending this email so that everyone knows exactly what's going on regarding my illness. I'm sure you can appreciate that it's pretty distressing telling people bad news over the phone, and I didn't want anyone to feel like they were the last to know. So here it is:

I was originally diagnosed with Acute Lymphoblastic Leukaemia in September 1998. I was treated at Boston Pilgrim, Grantham and Nottingham City hospitals. After achieving remission I moved to London to finish my degree and had follow up maintenance treatment at Greenwich District Hospital. When this hospital closed my care was transferred to the new Queen Elizabeth Hospital in Woolwich. In April of this year I suffered a relapse, and after some chemotherapy at

Woolwich I went to University College Hospital (UCH) London for my bone marrow transplant. This happened on July 20th, and I was discharged in early August. Everything seemed to be going fine and many of you have seen me out and about in the last few weeks. Most of you are already aware of all this.

On Sunday night I felt a twinge in my back. This became progressively worse, but I convinced myself it was just a muscle sprain. As you may know, back pains have been the first indicator of both my previous incidences of leukaemia. On Tuesday 30th October I had a bone marrow sample taken as I was 100 days post transplant. The results came through this morning (Wednesday) and Doctor Carl Pegg called me to let me know that they were not good. He informed that my bone marrow aspirate was showing an unusually high number of 'blasts' (as in 'lymphoblasts'), too many to just be after-transplant niggles. On his advice my parents and I drove down to UCH to see him this afternoon.

At UCH Dr Pegg told me that 30% of my bone marrow cells are showing as cancerous. The transplant itself was successful, but the chemotherapy and radiotherapy had not been sufficient to prevent the leukaemia from returning. There was always a chance of this. We knew this from the outset. If left alone the cancerous cells would flood my bone marrow and in a matter of weeks I would no longer be able to produce enough healthy cells to stay alive. My only option is to have another course of chemotherapy. This will provide a 20-30% chance of achieving remission.

Unfortunately, even if I achieve remission, the leukaemia will almost certainly return within a year. If it does then more chemotherapy, this time with an even lesser chance of remission, will be required. Not only will the chances of remission be lower, but the poisonous effects of the chemotherapy will be greater.

There is no longer any talk of curing my leukaemia. Both preferred options of care have been tried, and both have failed. Another transplant is not an option, as my body would not withstand the rigours of the transplant process so soon after the last, and even if one was to be carried out at a later date, the leukaemia itself would not be cured. The talk now is of merely prolonging my life.

I asked if I would ever have a 'normal' life with a career and so on. The answer was no. In all likelihood I have a year or maybe two left to live.

I have decided to keep my care at UCH. I will begin my chemotherapy on Monday. From now on I will be living each day as it comes.

Please don't be afraid to email or call.

Jon

Editor's Note

Jonathan's email 'Bad news in full' unsurprisingly generated a huge response from friends and loved ones. This is a sampling of those emails, along with Jonathan's replies.

1/11/01

Hi Jon

So sorry to read your news. You tried everything you could so well do. You have an amazing spirit and I'm sure you, your doctors and your family will make things as comfortable as possible for you. I really can't imagine your thoughts and feelings at the moment.

Joy.

2/11/01

Hi Joy

I'm not actually in any physical discomfort at the moment, so I'm just enjoying myself this weekend before I go back to hospital and not trying to think too much about what lies ahead. I bought myself a Playstation 2, so that should prove some distraction!

1/11/01

I'm having a hard time writing this email. I am writing things and deleting everything and starting over. I am struggling with what I 'want' to say and what I 'should' say. My emotions are mixed in am jacked up way...

Mike Woodburn

3/11/01

Hey.

Thanks for the email man. You know how much I appreciate the way you and all my friends have kept in touch, regardless of continental divides or different time zones. It means a lot to me to have such strong support...

So it's Guy Fawkes weekend at the moment. I'm sure you know the whole deal about our wacky British Bonfire Night celebrations. Anyway we're having a big fire and fireworks in my parents' back garden. Should be cool, most of the crew are here...
I'll speak to you soon my man.
Thanks again for everything.

Jon.

01/11/01
I cannot see you giving up on this... I don't know how you are feeling right now, but I know myself and many others marvelled at your resolve when you were first hit with the news and I know that's the person you are.
Graham

2/11/01
Hey Graham thanks for your email. I don't really have time to write a full reply right now, but I just wanted to say that I appreciate your support, and I hope you keep in touch.

It's weird but in some ways the news that I didn't get on to the course at Leeds upset me more immediately than the news about my health. I was really looking forward to moving oop north.
Jon

14/11/01
It has been nearly two weeks now since I received your last email. There has not been a day that has gone by when I haven't thought about what I was going to say. I just did not know how to express myself without either sounding like a morose idiot or an insensitive fool.
Richard.

17/11/01
Thanks for mailing. I'm out of hospital at the moment which is

good – enjoying spending some time with my family. I'll hopefully have another week or two at home before I have any more treatment. Hoping to get away at the end of the year, maybe on a big family vacation (first time we've been together in years) possibly Vegas!

Like I say I'm back in Grantham at the moment, but give me a call in a couple of weeks and come and see me at UCH.

OCTOBER 31ST 2001

During the morning Nursery session I was asked to go to the school office to answer a telephone call. At the time I thought it was nothing more than an inconvenience.

> *'Hello, Brenda Kay Nursery class teacher speaking.'*
> *'Brenn, it's Peter. We've had bad news. Blasts have been found in Jon's bone marrow. The hospital want to see us this afternoon.'*

It was day 98 after the transplant. All had been going well. So well in fact that Jonathan was planning a trip to the Grand Canyon.

I put down the phone and just sobbed. Hope was lost. For the first time in all those hours, days, weeks, months and years, hope was lost.

Friends took over. I was bundled in a car and driven home. I walked in through the front door. Jonathan stood there. What could I say? You can't say anything. Words really aren't enough.

We drove to UCH one more time. On arrival, we were informed that 'Jon's' room, room 11, was ready and that Dr Karl Pegg would be along to speak to us shortly. The house-keeper arrived with a tray of tea and biscuits. Not the ordinary tray to welcome visitors but a deluxe version with two doilies and the best biscuits. I knew then that we were in for bad news. Two doilies could only ever mean bad news.

Jonathan sat in the chair, Dr Karl on the bed. He explained that because blasts had been found it meant that the leukaemia had returned. Worse, the blasts were rapidly multiplying. There was nothing more to be done. Jonathan was terminally ill.

For the very first time I saw Jonathan cry. It broke my heart. I couldn't bear to look at him or my husband. Dr Karl informed us that ironically the transplant had been a success. Jonathan's body had accepted Thomas' bone marrow. It was just that the Leukaemia had returned for the third time. We had done everything we could, but it wasn't enough.

Jonathan had choices to make. He could do nothing and make the most of his limited time left or he could opt for a treatment called FLAG[34], which may buy him some extra time but would not cure him.

FLAG would be both unpleasant and painful, something Jonathan was all too familiar with. Despite this, Jonathan agreed to give it a go. He made only one request: Was there time for him to pop down to HMV on Oxford Street to buy a Play Station Two?

We all went, and just before closing time Jonathan got his Play Station.

We called in again to PPW2 to confirm arrangements. FLAG would commence the following Monday. Jonathan was advised to make the most of the forthcoming weekend.

The journey out of London was horrendous. We hit rush hour, and there were road works everywhere. It was dark, cold, and large drops of rain lashed against the windscreen. Over an hour later we were still stuck in traffic. I suggested we stop for a break. It was a relief to get out of the car. Jonathan led us to nearby coffee bar. We sat at the table in silence. Jonathan lit up a cigarette.

'No bloody point in giving up, was there?'

I select the biggest, most calorific, creamy, chocolaty, piece of gateau available. It tastes like cardboard, but I still manage to down the lot!
We get home. At first everyone walks on eggshells, but Jonathan snaps us out of the dismal mood by announcing that he would like to host a Bonfire party for his friends. Peter is very keen on this idea, he likes fireworks. He spends an exorbitant amount.

While out, he's also purchased The Guardian *(November 1st 2001) and there in the Technology section on the letters page published for all to see is a letter written by Jonathan. He finally got his letter in* The Guardian.

---

34 Abbreviation for a group of chemotherapy drugs.

The weekend goes so quickly, too quickly. I pack yet again. Time to return to London.

⁂   ⁂   ⁂

So here we are again, back on PPW2. Things are much the same as before. We quickly slip into 'our' routine. The days go by, we talk about anything and everything.

Everything that is except the things that we should talk about: what's going to happen at the end? What does he want for his funeral?.

One afternoon I make the HUGE mistake of saying I wish that it could have been me who was ill. Jonathan becomes extremely angry. I can't remember what was said because I was in tears. I flee from the room. When I return I find Jonathan with his head out of the window smoking a cigarette. He carefully stubs the cigarette out taking heed of the 1960's notice that is part of the window frame, 'Please do not throw cigarette ends out of this window'. He turns to face me, that slow easy smile spreads across his face. All is forgiven, because what else can we do?

Throughout the treatment Jonathan is confined to his room. I have been part of the ward for so long that people regard me as part of the staff. The two little old ladies who share a room further down the corridor often ask if I will make them a cup of tea!

The nurses now refer to me as Vigilante Mum after my part in identifying a 'suspicious character'. This individual had been stealing from hospital patients and staff. He had evaded capture for several weeks. He was also suspected of arson in several hospitals. One day, I was watching television in the Day Room when I noticed him in the stairwell. I asked if he was lost. He replied that he was looking for PPW3. I gave him directions, but when he walked up the stairs, his body language was all off. I alerted the nurses, and he was captured. His pockets were stuffed with mobile phones, purses and wallets. The little shit!

Later on, I hear frantic banging on the door of my room. It's David, one of the nurses.

> *'Come quickly, Jonathan's trashing his room, and we can't calm him down.'*

I enter the room. The contents of the wardrobe are strewn across the floor.

    'Wallet!' screams Jonathan. 'Where the fuck's my wallet?'
    'It's here son in the pocket of your new jeans.'

I place the wallet in his hand. He calms down. David says the staff had been concerned by the depth of his anger, his violence and rage. They were thankful his Mum had been there to deal with the situation. I was thankful to that he had released all those pent up feelings and emotions.

It comes as a relief to everyone when we're allowed to go home for the weekend.

Jonathan was sitting on the settee engrossed in the Sunday papers. Sensing something wasn't quite right, I approached him thermometer in hand.

    'Go away, stop fussing.'
    'Just let me check.'
    'No, stop fussing.'

Things continued like this for a couple of hours. Finally, he relented. His temperature had risen slightly. An hour later it had risen even more. The next check showed another rise. He had to have immediate medical attention. We made some arrangements: I would drive him to the local A and E, and UCH would call them clarifying the treatment that Jonathan would require.

We were met by a nurse and immediately shown into a cubicle. Forty-five minutes later we were still waiting to be seen by a doctor! I had already asked three times where the doctor was, only to be fobbed off. By this time Jonathan had started shaking. His condition was deteriorating. I ventured down the corridor only to hear the staff laughing and joking over a cup of coffee. I was furious! We had been told that immediate medical attention was necessary but none had been forth coming.

Marching into the room I made my intentions very clear: who was the doctor in charge and why had no one been to examine my son? The reply was that because Jonathan was neutropenic, which meant his immune system was barely functioning, and the doctor had a bit of a cold, so he couldn't do anything.

    'Do you understand what's happening?'

This made me see red. I was so, so angry. My son was terminally ill. He was deteriorating before my eyes and this patronising, arrogant prat sat there drinking coffee!

> *'Yes, I fully well understood what's happening: You're doing nothing! It is imperative that Jonathan have immediate medical attention and if that does not happen I will hold this hospital totally accountable."*

By now Jonathan was in a mess. He was having one rigor after another, and his temperature was extremely high. In short, he was fighting for his life.

We were transferred into a single room. It was the early hours of the morning. My son was dying before my eyes, and the people here were running around like headless chickens.

Things got worse when the door burst open and in came a doctor. He was cursing UCH, how dare they phone him and tell him how to treat a patient? Who did they think they were? Now this person should have had WASSAK tattooed in very large letters across their forehead.

As a general rule of thumb, in all of our many dealings with the medical profession we had found that the louder and more opinionated the individual, the lower their skills.

The Wassak, as I shall call him, marched up to Jonathan and began to access his Hickmann Line, continuing his verbal tirade. I went straight for the jugular.

> *'Doctor' (the word stuck in my throat) 'seeing as my son is nutropenic, would it not have been prudent to wash your hands before you touched his Hickmann Line?'*

I spoke these words slowly and carefully in the tone of voice of a mother who was scarier than God. The Wassak left the room.

So did I. I'd had enough. It was like taking part in a pantomime. My frustration lay in that no one seemed to know what to do. I could understand this – they most probably had never come across a patient undergoing FLAG before and might never do so again for a number of years – but the refusal to accept and act upon the advice from UCH, no way.

I called UCH and spoke to the ward sister of PPW2.

> *'What would happen if I insisted Jonathan returned to London?'*
> *'You'll kill him.'*

Returning to the room, I was informed that Jonathan would be moved to intensive care. UCH had been on the phone again. Strategies had been put into place. At last.

I expected ICU to be calm and controlled. I was wrong. Phones rang, the staff chatted loudly at the nurses station while drinking and eating, and there was a constant stream of visitors. Yet another doctor approached me. Her manner suggested that my reputation for being a difficult relative had gone before me. I got that slow-talking-doctor voice:

> *'Mrs Kay, you will wait in the relatives room whilst we insert a catheter into your son and begin his treatment.'*
> *'Why are you inserting a catheter?'*
> *'Because it is hospital procedure.'*
> *'No, I asked why.'*
> *'When a patient arrives in ICU, we always insert a catheter.'*
> *'My son is no ordinary patient. He is neutropenic and by inserting a catheter you are introducing a possible site for infection. I want to know why you need to do this.'*
> *'It's hospital procedure.'*
> *'I'm not satisfied. I insist you speak to UCH.'*
> *'We don't need to. He's our patient.'*
> *'Oh, no, he's my son, and I will hold this hospital totally accountable if you do not speak to UCH.'*

I won. That magic phrase says so much, and there was no way I was going to lose. I was fighting for Jonathan to be with me a little longer. I wasn't ready to let him go. After all we had been through, he was not going to die on account of some pig-headed individuals not having the common sense to make use of a invaluable source of advice.

The next step was to remove me to the relative's room.

The staff gathered en masse: a senior doctor, a junior doctor, a staff nurse and the Macmillan Nurse. Safety in numbers?

I remained outwardly calm. They began the conversation by stating they understood I was a little upset and rather emotional about what was happening. Emotional! I was angry more than anything else, but I did not resort to swearing or losing my temper. I had merely channelled my energies into becoming assertive. The conversation continued:

> *'Do you understand Jonathan is terminally ill? Do you know what terminally ill means? Do you understand he might die?'*

I wish I was making this up. Yes, of course, I understood all of that, but did they even begin to comprehend my frustration in the fact that expert advice was on hand and that they were failing to use it?

They then instructed me to call Peter. They said Jonathan was dying and that he was not expected to live more than an hour or two.

I sat by Jonathan's bedside holding his hand. He was a mass of wires, many of which were linked up to monitors displaying various numbers and coloured lines. These 'pinged' incessantly. My feelings were so mixed: my emotions in a turmoil but I had to remain calm and controlled since so much was at stake. Jonathan turned to me.

> *'Mum, look. I'm a robot.'*
> *'It's ok, son, they're just to monitor your progress. Hang in there.'*

Sometime later, a wave of calm swept over the unit. The ICU consultant and the Haematology consultant (Dr Tringham) had arrived. They were immediately joined by several doctors and nurses. The group disappeared in order to confer and make decisions concerning Jonathan's care. I was relieved that Dr T was there. Now the ship had a Captain, someone to take overall control of the situation, things would happen.

Dr T came to us and got straight to the point.

> *'I've spoken to UCH. The first thing we need to do is to insert a catheter.'*
> *'Why?'*

I got a swift kick in the ankle from my husband for that.

> *'Jonathan's failed to pass urine.'*

'That's incorrect, Dr T. He passed urine last night in A and E and again early this morning in the side room. Don't you remember Dr Wassak? I asked if you needed to test it.'

Extra hard kick from husband.

'In fact he's just passed urine again, and I asked the nurse to label the bottle when she placed it in the sluice.'

My reputation as the relative form hell was fully warranted! I had learnt a great deal on PPW2. Dr T was magnificent.

'In that case there's no need to insert a catheter.'

The worst was over. At long last Jonathan's treatment was both appropriate and on schedule. Contact with London was frequent. Progress was meticulously monitored on a huge chart. We often glanced at that chart but couldn't begin to understand it. What we could understand was that Jonathan was making progress, that there was the possibility that he could regress but there was the much stronger possibility that he would make it.

Visitors came and went. Many, especially Jonathan's friends and brothers were shocked by his appearance. They found the technology all too much. It was a stark reminder to all of us that we had a great deal to be thankful for.

On the Wednesday Jonathan returned to UCH by ambulance. He rode 'shotgun' for the last part of the journey directing the driver through the traffic to the hospital. He walked on to PPW 2 greeting the staff with 'Hello I'm back'.

I journeyed down by train. The first thing I did when I arrived on the ward was to check that Jonathan was ok. Then I went to my room and slept. It was the first time in four days that I had been able to relax.

Jonathan made light of it all. His only regret was that he had returned to London in an ambulance and not a helicopter. He commented that would have enjoyed landing in Tottenham Court Road and being whisked ER style into the hospital building! As if we hadn't had enough drama!

Email to Chris – 8/12/01

Hey Chris

Yes I'm back in Grantham at the moment. I've been in and out of the local hospital to have top ups of blood and platelets. It was mental actually – the other night I was having an overnight blood transfusion and my dad was with me in the room. His phone rang and it turned out that one of my younger brothers Chris was on his way into casualty as "one of his mates had run him over". We went round to casualty and there he was being stretchered in. Thing is Chris is 6'5" and must weigh like 16 stone at least so in fact his mate's car kind of came off worse. Chris had a sprained knee and bruised fingers plus a small bump on the head. The car has a buckled bumper, crumpled bonnet and cracked windscreen.

I'll be in London on Thursday for a bone marrow test, but I'm not anticipating hanging around to be honest. I will make sure we all meet up in the big smoke before Xmas. I have been out and about a bit – I went to see Alkaline Trio in Leicester on Monday night, which I enjoyed but I found it very tiring.

Gone a bit crazy with the credit card- bought myself a new acoustic guitar (I've been guitarless for six months and its been painful). Then the other night I ordered myself a whole new hi-fi separates set-up on line – £550 including £65 just on cables and interconnects! Can't wait for that lot to turn up. And I've decided that I'm going to have a full sleeve tattoo done (Hey, it's not like I have to worry about job interviews anymore is it?)

See you soon.
Jon.

CHRISTMAS 2001

Christmas will soon be upon us. I write cards and buy presents. I go to Oxford Street with a friend and shop for England. We get as far as Tottenham Court Road, stop for lunch and drink far too much wine. I'm sloshed. My speech is slurred and my movements are uncoordinated, but this does not prevent me from finding my way back to PPW2. It feels good to let go for a couple of hours.

Jonathan's treatment is relentless, even when we return to Grantham, we still have to report to the local hospital.

The festive preparations are going well. Jonathan announces that he's got all of his shopping done thanks to Amazon and the net. He then proceeds to spend most of his time challenging others to beat his score on any Play Station Two game. The competition is fierce. The sight of him sitting with his friend Jamie scoring points off one another brings tears to my eyes. Jonathan has never become melancholy, never wallowed in self-pity. If anything he's the strong one supporting his friends and family by keeping everything 'normal'.

What to do on Christmas Day is a difficult decision. Jonathan provides the solution. He wants to spend the day at home doing all the things that we have always done as a family: hanging up the home made Christmas sacks, eating chocolate money before breakfast, opening our presents together and turkey for lunch. We all strive to make it the best Christmas ever, while still trying to pretend it's all absolutely fine.

The traditional Boxing Day family gathering in Derby is quite an ordeal. No one really knows what to do or say. The children keep us all entertained, but somehow their presence highlighted what was not to be. I couldn't wait to leave.

I almost broke down the next day when we went to have a family portrait taken by a local photographer. I tried so hard to smile through the tears, but I was unable to stop them from falling. I hadn't truly realised how frail Jonathan has become until I see the photos.

Email – 30/12/01

Christmas has been good. I got some new robots (two dancing, one clockwork and one that has an operation style tweezer extraction game built into it). Oh and I also got a Japanese robot fish from Tony who just got back from Tokyo. When our garden pond thaws I'm going to see how well the mechanized terror fish interacts with my Dad's goldfish. I'm hoping that they will swim away scared then seven seconds later forget what it was that they were scared of and swim straight back towards the jaws of doom, then swim away again in a never ending cycle of fear.

Going back to hospital on the 3rd of January. Not looking forward to it, but best to get it out of the way whilst the weather is so shitty. I was given a Hives ticket for February 7th (at the mighty Rock City, Nottingham) so that's my target for recovery.

See you soon,
Love
Jon.

JANUARY 2002

We return to UCH for more treatment. January is cold, grey, and dismal, like it always is. It's a struggle to get out of bed in the morning. The 'slow' days, without any treatment are filled with apathy. Our mood is as dismal as the weather and the prospect of spending each and every day in one room hangs heavy on us. We both accept that it is something we have to get through, have to endure, but boredom rapidly sets in. Visitors and phone calls are very few and far between.

Nothing seems to hold our interest. Jonathan barely glances at The Guardian. I'm certain I've seen every TV programme, read every book. I suggest that we play Scrabble to pass the time. Jonathan refuses, 'God, are we really that desperate?'

During November Jonathan had proof-read our friend Carol's dissertation for her M.A. This had absorbed his attention as he wrote numerous comments in red pen all over her work. The only page that he deemed perfect was one that she had left blank by mistake! How I longed for something like that now to occupy the time.

At least I can venture out. I walk up and down Tottenham Court Road buying the most stupid items in the sales. Topics of conversation became so limited that I resort to giving Jonathan progress reports concerning the homeless person who appears to be living in a car outside the hospital.

I also spend a great deal of time talking to the staff. Most – Barry, Javi, David, Gemma and Gill – have become good friends. They comfort me when it all gets too much. It's a big help.

There is one nurse I avoid. She seems obsessed by death. It's all she wants to talk about. She bears a strong resemblance to a vampire and is working on a haematology ward! Perhaps I should buy some garlic.

Ward rounds are done by a regular team of doctors Jonathan likes: Karl, Emma, Mark and Lux. He'll eagerly challenge them regarding his treatment. There is a mutual respect there. Such is the rapport that he will discuss the problems he's having regarding controlling his bowel movements. Frequently his pants are soiled and he's embarrassed. When I offer to wash them he gets angry. It's unavoidable, though. He must take the medication; the medication produces side effects. The team strive to correct the balance.

At one stage the diarrhoea becomes quite a problem. Jonathan has managed to soil his pants and jeans. The ward washing machine is jammed with a load that I put in earlier. The door stuck. It's two days later and we're still waiting for Household Maintenance to arrive. I dash down to Oxford Street, run into M&S, buy six pairs of pants, dash back to UCH, fling the pants at Jonathan, then dash back out to find a launderette. Armed with a black plastic bag full of 'undesirable items', I find one quite easily. Dot Cotton is even there clad in obligatory nylon overall. She's a real gem, though, and before too long I am leaving the establishment with a bag of items clean enough to pass the Daz doorstep challenge!

Jonathan develops and infection and because of the implications for other patients he is moved to the Patrick Mansen Unit on the other side of the hospital. This makes matters worse. He becomes more surly and withdrawn. Without our usual nurses to talk to the days seem longer than ever.

I am relieved that the 24th is getting nearer. I've planned to go to Bournemouth for the weekend with a group of friends. I can't wait. I really need a break. Dare I say it from Jonathan – I know he needs a break from me!

SATURDAY JANUARY 25TH 2002

We had spent a 'carefree' (ha!) day in Bournemouth with our friends. The boys (David, Christopher and Thomas) had been to London to visit Jonathan. They said they found him in good spirits, up and dressed, and there was even talk of Jonathan being well enough to move back to PPW2 later in the week if his chest infection cleared. Leaving Jonathan reading the paper, his brothers went shopping, promising to call back about 3 o'clock before they got the train home.

When they returned, they spent a good half hour laughing and joking with one another. Then Jonathan stood up to go to the toilet and fainted. They picked him up off the floor, got him back on the bed and called the nurse. Jonathan began to have a rigor, shaking uncontrollably. I'm not sure what happened after that. The boys have never really talked about it, other than to say it was frightening.

Peter and I received a phone call from the hospital at about 6 o'clock, asking us to return to London as soon as possible. I have very little recall of the journey back from Bournemouth, other than it was pelting with rain and the windscreen wipers squeaked each time they crossed the windscreen. We didn't speak at all on that journey.

When we go to his room, Jonathan was lying on the floor, surrounded by doctors and nurses. It was like walking on to the set of a medical drama. MY son, fighting for his life. There were tubes everywhere, all seemingly connected to a very large orange bag. Despite the severity of the situation there was an organised calm about it all, which was reassuring. Each medic had a clearly defined role, and they were all working together. The doctor in charge explained that Jonathan was in septic shock and that, as bad as it looked, they felt he was now stable enough to move down to Intensive Care.

So Jonathan was taken down to ICU, and we were asked to wait in the relative's room. What a dog hole! It was so dirty there was even a half-eaten meal left on the table. We waited and waited and waited, in silence, staring at the dirty marks on the floor. Eventually we were asked to accompany the medical team into an adjacent office. Sitting down was a problem as there weren't enough chairs and every surface was littered with piles of papers. Jeff the consultant entered. He had 'presence' and really inspired confidence. This eased the stress a little. Funny how something as simple as competence can do that.

Jeff calmly explained that Jonathan was on the brink of death, they were doing what they could, but that things did not look good. The septicaemia was ravaging Jonathan's body. There was a course of action open: intubate Jonathan, put him on a breather, keeping him essentially in a plastic bubble. It would probably keep Jonathan alive a little longer, but it meant he was unlikely that he would ever leave ICU. The situation was that grave.

Peter said we had to keep him alive at all costs.

'NO!' I shouted. 'NO, NO, NO!' I took my husband's hands

and looked into his eyes. 'Peter, let him go. His body is riddled with cancer. His lungs are knackered. Love him, let him go, let him die with dignity. He's done so well, fought so long, but don't prolong the agony. He deserves better than being hooked up to a machine that will breathe for him.'

Jeff the specialist left the room. He came back saying he had been to see Jonathan who had indicated through sign language that he did not want to be intubated[35]. Do Not Resuscitate had been written on his notes.

Peter and I held hands as we walked nervously into the unreal world of ICU. Jonathan was in the corner, in a special unit which had glass sides. It was necessary to wash your hands and wear a plastic apron before you went in. He was lying there with tubes coming out of the jugular vein in his neck, wires everywhere and machines bleeping all around him.

'Hello love, hang on in there. We're here now.'

God, how much more can he take?

---

35 Intubation is where a patient would be sedated, and a tube be inserted in to the patient's mouth. A ventilator would breathe on his behalf. In Jonathan's condition, he would have been unlikely ever to recover from this. He almost certainly would have realised the implications of this.

GLASS BOX

My memories of sitting in that glass box hour after hour, day after day are very muddled.

ICU is a strange place. It's a timeless, dull, quiet world where everything is in limbo, suspended in time. There is little for a parent to do or say. The nurses move quietly, attending every possible need. Their calm approach is unnerving and soothing at the same time.

It is so difficult to know what to do or say.

I sit there holding Jonathan's hand telling him 'Well done, son', 'Keep fighting', 'You're making progress, keep going', but what kept sticking in my mind was how much I hated the salmon pink scrubs they'd dressed him in. The colour just didn't suit him!

Each mouthful of water is a triumph, each drop of build-up drink a victory. At times the drugs make him delirious. He rambles on and on, becoming angry if we don't answer his questions. There's a funny moment when Jonathan asks to see his bag of urine from the catheter. His response? 'Wow!'

Amazingly, he pulled through the worst. After a few days, he was able to sit up in bed and hold a conversation. At one point he asked us to read him the clues from The Guardian crossword, which he then completed. Friends came to visit, and many of staff from PPW2 also called in after their shifts. One night, Gill, a nurse from PPW2, arrived with Javi, one our favourite nurses. Javi looks exactly like Jesus Christ, so Gill made him wear a very loud t-shirt just in case Jonathan woke up suddenly and thought he'd finally met his maker.

Jonathan still needed a face-mask to help him breathe, but by the sixth day things appeared to be going according to plan. Peter even returned home. Sitting around in hospitals is not a man's thing. The boys arranged to come and see Jonathan during the next week. I stayed in London. Even though things were looking up, no matter how hard I tried I couldn't shake off a feeling of gloom.

On Tuesday morning, I walk into the unit. All the team are present, standing in a circle outside Jonathan's room. Their eyes meet mine.

> '*It's ok. I know he's dying, only got two or three days left.*'

A doctor we took to calling Clinical Bitch speaks first.

> '*Of course, we're not going to tell him. He needn't know.*'

Stupid cow! She had been part of the team caring for Jonathan for the past eight months and had never developed a rapport with him. She was too clinical, too cold. Patients were just names and hospital numbers, not people with feelings. I tell her she must tell Jonathan, but she refuses. Which leaves it up to me.

I sit by the bed and hold Jonathan's hand.

> '*It's not good news, son. The tests are showing that things aren't going well. The Leukaemia is spreading and the infection is taking a stronger and stronger hold. I'm going to send for Dad.*'

> '*Stop being so melodramatic, Mum. I know. I feel as if my lungs are playing catch up with my heart, but that's all*'.

I try to put my arms around him, but he screams in pain and turns away. I run from the room.

By the time I'm back on PPW2 to get to my room, the tears are flowing. Barry, another nurse close to us, appears. I tell him that I can't bear to see Jonathan die in intensive care. It's so impersonal and cold. Barry says he'll see what he can do. I seek out Dr Emma hoping she'll talk to Jonathan and tell him the truth. I trust her – she's one of the best.

Peter arrives. We go to sit with Jonathan. Peter refuses to believe what I have told Jonathan. They gang up on me. I leave in tears. It takes a couple of hours for me to calm down. By the time I return to ICU Dr Emma has been. Jonathan's reaction is anger and frustration.

'Bugger, now I'll never see the next Star Wars *sequel.'*

A distant friend of Jonathan's enters. He begins by apologising that he has not been to visit. Lame excuses are offered. Jonathan informs him that it is a good job he made the effort to visit today because he only has another two to three days to live. Silence. Chilling silence. What do you say to that?

WEDNESDAY 6TH FEBRUARY
Barry has pulled a few strings and arranged for Jonathan to be moved back on to the Patrick Mansen Unit. In addition, he's ensured that Javi will attend to Jonathan over night.

Waiting to be moved is an ordeal. There is a new doctor in ICU and yet another new nurse for Jonathan. The doctor speaks to the nurse first. They both consult Jonathan's notes. The doctor reaches out with her index finger and points to Do Not Resuscitate. The nurse looks at her and smiles as if they are sharing some secret. Their manner makes me so angry, but I resist the urge to jump up and slap their smug faces. What good will it do?

Jonathan is moved. The strain almost kills him. I can't stop crying. Jonathan tells me 'to go away and don't come back until you can bloody well stop'! I return to PPW2, make a coffee and sit in the Day Room watching a television programme about a couple trying to set up a hotel business. The couple have had to face problems and various hardships and are worried about coping with the stress of it all. GET REAL! GET A LIFE! HOW DOES MAKING A BUSINESS SUCESSFUL COMPARE TO LOSING YOUR CHILD??

Later, I call in to kiss Jonathan good night. What will tomorrow bring?

THURSDAY 7TH FEBRUARY 2002

I hear Peter leaving our room at PPW2 very early in the morning. I roll over in bed and pretend to be asleep. Perhaps if I pretend hard enough I can convince myself that none of this is really happening. It's a forlorn hope. The phone rings.

> *'Brenn, come over. He hasn't got much longer.*

I throw on some clothes, find my spectacles (no time for contact lenses today), and rush out. As I run the gauntlet of heroin addicts in A&E I can't help thinking: Why not one of them? WHY? WHY? WHY?

I enter the room. Barry and Javi are there. Javi walks over and gives me a hug. It helps. Jonathan is struggling to breathe. Barry tells me that Jonathan has told Javi during the night that he's ready to die. Dr Emma has been sent for and will prescribe what's needed to make Jonathan most comfortable.

We need to phone the boys. Thomas was getting the 7.30am from Scarborough and then meeting David and Christopher in Grantham, so they could all come down and say goodbye.

But it's too late.

Once again I hold Jonathan's hand and we talk. Memories, precious memories. Dr Emma comes in. She holds Jonathan's other hand and tells him what will happen. She's crying as she leaves the room.

Peter talks to Jonathan. I stare at the newspaper, letting Peter have his final chat. Barry leans over and very carefully takes the paper away from me, folding it up precisely. He explains that Jonathan is taking his last breaths, but that hearing is the last sense to go. We should both keep talking to him.

> *'Go to sleep, son. Time to rest. We love you.'*
> *'Love you,' Jonathan says.*

These are his last words. He dies a few seconds later at 10.15 am. I kiss him gently. The time has finally come to let go. Jonathan always had an all or nothing attitude to life, and now he's given life his all.

I'm numb. I have no experience with death. I've never even seen a dead person before. Barry comes to our aid. He suggests we see to some of the practicalities. This is far from insensitive. It is, in fact, a great comfort. It's part of the grieving process to tie up of loose ends.

My task is to find Jonathan some clothes to wear. I choose his favourite t-shirt and a pair of new jeans from Harrods. When I return to the room Barry and another nurse, Nancy, are washing Jonathan. They ask if I would like to help and then help to dress him. It's a lovely gesture, but I'm suddenly scared, scared of not being able to move stiff limbs, scared that I would hurt him. Jonathan has also always been very private about his body. I have no desire to invade his privacy or demean his dignity. I'm finally able to utter a pitiful 'no'.

Barry senses my dilemma and says exactly the right thing.

> *'It's okay. I have Nancy here to help me.'*

He also says that the staff of PPW2 had been so fond of Jonathan that many had asked if they could do this last thing for him, this washing and dressing of him. Jonathan has been special to more than just me. I lean forward and kiss his lips. His skin feels warm and clammy.

> *'Sleep well, my darling. I love you always.'*

We collect the death certificate from a gloomy little room somewhere in the depths of the hospital. The lady who works there is such a kind and helpful person. She explain that we have to go to Camden Town Hall to register the death. She also explains lots of other things, but I can't remember any of them.

Peter and I walk out of the hospital and through the streets. It's a lovely sunny day and the air is fresh. It feels like Spring. When we get to the Town Hall, we have a short wait before the Registrar shows us into a private room. Words come tumbling out of my mouth, and I found myself telling her all about Jonathan and the three and a half years that he had spent fighting Leukaemia. She writes out the certificate, only pausing once to wipe a tear from her eye.

After tidying our room and saying farewell to the staff we finally leave PPW2. Our journey home is not easy, but we make it. Facing the boys is the hardest part. The look in their eyes is the same as mine.

I sit on the settee exhausted. One of the cats clambers onto my knee. As I stroke her, I can hear Jonathan's voice in my head.

'Stop bloody crying, and get on with it!'

This is what I shall aim to do.

THE CELEBRATION

When I finally wake on the Friday morning I struggle to recall where I am, and for one brief moment my mind cons me into believing it's all been a bad dream. I go into the bathroom in a daze, hoping beyond hope that, in true soap opera style Jonathan, will emerge from the shower.

But he doesn't, of course. They never do.

The next few days are a blur. Our first task is to organise the funeral. The undertaker, Robert, is a friend of ours, which helps enormously. Everyone should be friends with an undertaker. We found ourselves sitting in his office, tissues in one hand, cups of coffee in the other, chatting politely about funeral cars and the price of coffins. This is the easy part.

We discuss the service. I've already outlined the proceedings in my head – years of organising assemblies at school have proved useful – and we already know Jonathan wanted to be cremated. So Robert phones the crematorium to book a slot. We choose February 14th, St Valentine's Day, at 2 o'clock. The order of service is intended to be regarded as a celebration of Jonathan's life and achievements. Robert suggests a non-religious format that provides a framework we can all work from.

Things take shape. Kathy Daszkievwicz will read a poem that she's written about Jonathan, Peter will say a few words and perhaps Andy or Jamie, Jonathan's closest friends, will also contribute. Robert will conduct the proceedings. The theme from Star Wars will play but not as the curtains closed. For that, an extract from Shakespeare might suffice. I suggest Jonathan's brothers and some of his friends can act as pall bearers, but Robert gently suggests this is 'not advisable'.

We briefly toy with the concept of an 'East End' type funeral with the horse and carriage, Robert in a top hat and frock coat and of course 'J-O-N' in big flowers, but we eventually decide it's too theatrical. Later, I'll occasionally wish we hadn't dismissed it, but that's what we decide to do.

133

Then, just as we're about to leave Robert's office, Peter says,

> *'What about a couple of hymns?'*
> *'WHAT?' I shriek. 'WHY?'*
> *'Well, it's sort of expected isn't it? What will people think?'*
> *'I DON'T CARE! This is Jonathan's funeral. He wouldn't want religion in any form and that's that. Who cares what people think?'*

Silence and tears follow. Robert, bless him, keeps his council, suggesting we can run through the proceedings again in a day or two.

On our return home there are yet more sympathy cards to open. In some ways I find these upsetting, but in other ways they do prove to be a great comfort. A double-edged sword. Many of our friends have written letters about Jonathan and their memories of him, it was obvious that he had made his mark. We also receive huge numbers of emails and phone calls. Even though he was terminally ill, everyone is shocked by Jonathan's death. We all got used to him fighting, and in some strange way I think many people expected he would have soldiered on for a lot longer.

Friends, neighbours and relatives call constantly or drop in to visit. Many bring flowers. We continue the theme: a tree is planted in the garden, and instead of a gravestone or plaque, we buy a piece of woodland dedicated to Jonathan's memory.

Everyone wants to do something to help, so after much discussion we decide hospitality will be offered at the house after the funeral. All our friends pitch in. Sue, Carol and Alison will make the sandwiches and serve the tea. Merrick will 'housesit' whilst we're all at the crematorium. And so on. Practicalities keep us sane. Peter occupies his time sorting out and purchasing the drinks. As we have no real idea of how many people will attend it's all guess- work. I spent a frustrating afternoon searching for paper serviettes; there is very little choice for 'funeral teas'.

Flowers turn into a drama. We decide on 'family flowers' only, with requests for donations to Leukaemia Research and UCH for friends and guests. I visualise a single bunch of 23 lilies on top of the coffin, but apparently it's the 'wrong time' for lilies. My second option, because the funeral is on St Valentine's Day is red roses. Locating 23 roses near Valentine's Day is not easy.

'It'll cost you,' says the florist
'So fucking what?,' I think, but hold my tongue.
'Flowers aren't that easy to arrange. You'll need lots of green stuff.'

Resisting the urge to punch Miss Unhelpful Shop Assistant of the Year right between the eyes, I keep calm. I assume my most assertive manner, honed with lots of practice on doctors, and explain in detail that I wanted to do this for Jonathan, that it's a personal thing, a final act of love? She's heard of love, hasn't she? I also assure her that it's not to 'do her out of a job' or to save me some money. Surely this cash register of a cow has a heart? She goes away to talk to the manager.

'He says he'll give you a bit of a discount, £72 for 24 roses'.

They're already priced at £3 each!!

'Or you can have 23 for £70.'

£1 extra profit to him! Didn't the moron think I could multiply and divide? What can you do? I'm beyond caring by this point, so I purchase the flowers, oasis and container and leave the shop.

My friend Sue provides the greenery free of charge! Hurray for small mercies! We plunder the bushes in her garden with great gusto. I return home armed with an abundance of foliage to fill in the gaps. Making the arrangement goes smoothly and I'm very pleased with the result. I cry as I place the roses, one for each year of Jonathan's life. I also spend a long time sorting through the photographs, putting together an album for people to look at after the funeral. It's meant to be a catalyst to prevent awkward silences.

Despite it being rather a busy week, we still have other commitments. Aunty Connie has died, too. On Monday, the day of her funeral, Peter disappears for a couple of hours, and it turns out he's bought me a new car!!! Obviously a man thing, something to do in the middle of all the chaos and confusion. MEN!

Aunty Connie's funeral goes by in a bit of a blur. The family tea-set makes an obligatory appearance along with a little 'old dear' who nobody knows sitting in a corner chomping her way through as many sandwiches and pieces of cake that she can manage.

And then, inevitably, THE day came. Most of the morning is spent tidying the house and setting up the bar. I lay out the tea set on a crisp white cloth and folded the serviettes. We're ready to receive our guests.

What to wear for your son's funeral? I choose the outfit that I'd worn for Jonathan's graduation. Peter wore a 'hand me up' shirt Jonathan had given to him. The boys faced a dilemma: shirts and ties or jeans and trainers. I said, whatever you feel most comfortable in; the day is difficult enough for all of us without imposing a dress code.

All too soon Robert knocks on the door. Time to go. My feet stick to the floor. All of a sudden, I can't move. This really is the last thing.

> *'Come on, Mum.'*

David takes me gently by the hand, and we walk out to the car. Each of us stares into space on the brief journey, not looking at one another, holding off crying until the last possible minute.

We arrive at the crematorium. There are people and cars everywhere. There's even a queue to get in!

> *'Busy day?' someone asked.*

Then it struck me: all these people were attending 'our' ceremony. There's Grandma, hobbling in on her walking sticks. There are many of Jonathan's mates. When I'll look back on this, I'll picture them all with skateboards, but that's probably not right. At the back of the queue I see Barry and Javi, Jonathan's last two nurses. In fact there are so many people present that a large group are going to have to stand outside the crematorium.

It's too much really. How can it not be? Grief washes over me again. I feel as if I'll drown in a sea of sorrow.

> *'Undo your seat belt.'*

Robert's calm words bring me back to the worst time and place of my life.

We've all come to celebrate Jonathan's life and that's what we do. The family sits in the front row. The boys concentrate on the floor. I tell them it's ok to cry.

The procession enters to Jonathan's favourite piece of music, Berber's Adagio for Strings, the theme from Platoon. *Robert welcomes everyone. He explains that the service will not be religious because that would not be in keeping with Jonathan's wishes and beliefs. Then Robert nods to the technician to play an extract from the theme to* Star Wars, *but the technician misunderstands and takes no notice. By the time the technician realises what's happening Peter is already at the podium and about to start! So the planned musical interlude is extremely short.*

Peter is amazing. Just amazing. He talks about Jonathan as a child, the young man that he had become and how proud we are of all that Jonathan achieved in his life. He talks about Jonathan's jobs and education and hopes and dreams. He tells jokes and funny things Jonathan said. He ends his speech with,

> *'During his last few days Jonathan asked me if I was as proud of him as he was of me. Of course I am. Proud of all the things he has achieved, of his intelligence and of his caring attitude. Proud of all the wonderful things his friends and acquaintances say about him. Goodbye Jonathan. May the force be with you.'*

We all laugh, and we all cry.

Kathy reads out her poem:

Jonathan

Your youngest brother will miss school on Monday.
He'll be screened at the haematology clinic
to see if his bone marrow matches yours.

Your Mum's floral notepaper, her ordinary script
are at odds with the stark news:
this week what was suspected was confirmed.

At sixteen you threw off school for college
and the uniform you'd complemented with a nose stud.
I'd turn a blind eye while the hole was raw.

I'd picture the slantwise scrawl of your essays
- grade A, but indecipherable, at times,
as the squiggles on a heart monitor. Recall that day.

you shaved your head. When I last saw you
at the station you tugged up a faded T-shirt
to shock me with your newly pierced navel.

Grey cells of cloud invade a clear stretch
of sky as I wander back from posting
the book I hope will make you laugh.

They looked at me oddly in Smith's
as I scanned each page anxious to ascertain
what the heroine's father died of.

Angina, in his sixties. At university your final year.
I bite my lip, try for another adjective.
And focus on the narrowing patch of blue.

Andy reads out an extract from Jonathan's writings in Fracture.

Robert takes over for the rest of the service and first reads out messages
from some people who knew Jonathan and couldn't be at the service:

David from Fracture*:*

Jon, thank you for being a part of *Fracture* for so long, and for
believing in what we were trying to do. Your columns always
struck a chord and I felt proud to have you in our pages. I only
met you a few times, but that was enough for me to realise what
an amazing person you were, and how lucky we were to have
you writing for us. You will be sorely missed in every way.

Jono Atkinson:

I am privileged to have known Jon.
Jon brought energy, life and enthusiasm.
Jon kept his energy despite everything he was forced to endure.
Jon's strength inspires me.....
Jon will always be with me.

Mike & Anna Woodburn, Mark D, Mike Calahan, Inzo, Pete Dawg,
Danny Boy, Mike Justice, Erik and Chris, Jonathan's friends in
California::

Let it be known that Jon is being thought of today thousands of
miles away as well as at home. In California, Jon's charisma,
intellect and sometimes biting wit made a lasting impression on

those of us he met. Not only was he immediately accepted as one of our own, but in time endeared himself to us as one of our true, real friends. And that's something that will live on through the rest of us. We'll always think of you, Jon, with a smile and a tear.

Robert says a few more words and another poem, and then all too soon it's the time when the curtains have to close. The music is 'Things Could Turn Around' by Firehose because Jonathan had told Andy that the lyrics had become his theme tune.

Then it's over. I have a moment of panic, unsure what to. Robert once again guides us gently by suggesting we walk outside.

As we stand there all these people keep coming one after another saying how special Jonathan was, how personal the proceedings have been and how much a mention of their name or an event they recalled had meant to them. There are so many of Jonathan's friends present, so many people who wanted to come.

When we get back home, there's a traffic jam outside the house. The one thing we forgot was that we would all arrive back at the house just as the school opposite would ring the home time bell. The men folk sprang into action as car park attendants.

My main recollections of the rest of the day are seeing those dammed teacups yet again and watching Jonathan's friends drinking beer, trying to look calm and relaxed. The photograph albums prove a good conversation point. We urge people to take one of Jonathan's books or robots as a keepsake but many politely decline. Perhaps it's too much too soon for them, or perhaps memories are all that you need when someone has given life their all.

*   *   *

It's still not over. 'Things' have not yet come to a final conclusion. Bank accounts have to be closed, student loans written off and passports returned. A glossy brochure arrives containing pictures of plaques, rose-trees and suggested suitable entries for a book of remembrance. As I glance at an extremely large marble obelisk, a voice spoke in my head,

> *'Is this what I'm reduced to? A phallic object in the middle of a field?'*

We choose not to collect the ashes or make an entry in the book. Instead, we decide as a family to remember Jonathan through his writings with the aim of inspiring others to give life their all.

And that's what you've been reading. So now I come to the end of my writing, and it's time for Jonathan to have the last word. It's what he would have insisted upon.

THE TOP OF THE HILL

Jonathan 'Shoes' Kay

I rode my brother's bike today, and I got half way up the hill behind my house.

Chemotherapy has ravaged my body. I weigh about three stones less than I did when I was diagnosed. I used to swim over a kilometre three times a week; now I struggle to walk into town. I used to be able to dunk a basketball; now I'd be lucky to make free throws. I am, however, getting stronger; a few months ago simply climbing the stairs in my house would leave me exhausted. On Brighton beach this weekend I was acutely aware of my atrophied arms and legs and embarrassed by my slight paunch. Chemotherapy has thrown me to the bottom of the hill, and it's time for me to start climbing it again.

One of the problems is that my year of near- immobility has (with the intake of toxic chemicals) reduced my appetite substantially. I have to force myself to eat in order to provide myself with the energy to even begin exercise. I had an appointment with the dietician at my hospital to discuss this problem. Unfortunately this took a while to arrange as the dietician was South African. I have a rather silly problem that I can't understand what South Africans say; I just hear the jarring tones of their accent. I can't focus on the words within it you see. So I rescheduled with one of her colleagues, and I was pleased to learn that I should eat plenty of ice cream and drink milkshakes in order to regain all that missing carbohydrates. Fine by me.

Being told to eat more, though, is not the blessing that it may first appear. A year of hospital food and appetite-suppressing drugs has made it extremely difficult for me to eat in any quantity. Every now and again I venture out to restaurants with friends and I get upset when I finish barely half the food on my plate. I need to eat more if I'm going to make it up the hill.

So I'm starting to eat a little more, but I had to face facts – I would have to begin a restorative programme of exercise. I wanted to go swimming, but schools almost continuously book up the crappy leisure centre in my hometown of Grantham. When it's not, it's packed with the denizens of the town. I'd like to play basketball but I have no friends here to play with. My hoop is out of action anyway. So I took to riding the bike, and I got half way up the hill.

I grew contemplative as I travelled through the bland scenery of South Kesteven. With the exception of the hill behind my house, which I got half way up, it is a flat desolate place. To paraphrase (or perhaps desecrate) Coleridge 'fields fields all around, and absolutely fuck all to do'.

I began to ruminate on the 'double burden' that myself and other cancer sufferers endure. The double burden is all the shit that you get on top of having leukaemia. For example: I told my bank I had leukaemia, they told me to cut up my credit cards. I guess they didn't want me to run up huge debts and then die. Or alternatively: I visited the USA 2 years ago and the cost of my insurance was around £50. Now, needing a holiday more than ever, I noticed the questions about 'pre-existing medical conditions' on the insurance forms. Most of the major insurers gave me a blanket 'no'. I rang a company that specialises in travel insurance for the 'medically dis-advantaged' (I love that term). Three weeks in the US? That'll be £265 mate. That's as much as my airfare! You can add to this the fact that I'm forced out of work and on to the dole. I've got no problem with taking welfare cheques, but I hate sitting around the house doing fuck all and getting a measly £39 a week for it. No I don't get any extra for the fact that I've got cancer. I didn't pay enough taxes to qualify for sickness ben-efit (stupid me, I went to university instead of getting a job at McDonalds!). I rode my bike, and they made the hill steeper.

So at the moment I'm halfway up the hill, and I can almost see the sum-mit. I need to persevere with the eating and the exercising, but I believe I can do it. I never gave much thought to the physical implications of my treatment when I was diagnosed. I was more concerned on the effect a year of hospital treatment and small town living would have on my intel-lect. Fortunately an incessant supply of reading material has helped keep the grey matter in check, and I've taken to writing with great voracity. It just remains for me to rebuild my emaciated form.

I rode my bike today, and I got half way up the hill. If I can make it to the top, then it's an easy ride back down.

USEFUL CONTACTS

Leukaemia Research
Leukaemia Research was established in 1960 and is still the only national research charity devoted exclusively to leukaemia, the lymphomas, myeloma, aplastic anaemia, myelodysplasia, the myeloproliferative disorders and the related blood disorders in both children and adults.
http://www.lrf.org.uk

Anthony Nolan Trust
Founded in 1974 as the first Register of volunteers willing to donate bone marrow in circumstances where a match cannot be found within a patient's family, The Anthony Nolan Trust now holds one of the largest databases of unrelated donors in the world.
http://www.anthonynolan.org.uk

Macmillan Cancer Relief
Macmillan Cancer Relief is a UK charity that works to improve the quality of life for people living with cancer
http://www.macmillan.org.uk

National Blood Service
Jonathan's treatment required frequent blood and platelet transfusions and the service relies on volunteers. "Do something amazing today – Save a life, Give blood".
http://www.blood.co.uk

Marie Curie Cancer Care
In the community, high-quality Marie Curie Nursing gives terminally ill people the choice of dying at home, supported by their families. There are 10 Marie Curie Hospices and the charity is also investigating the causes of cancer and better ways to treat the disease.
http://www.mariecurie.org.uk

OTHER LINKS

Brenda Kay
Mother of Jonathan. Visit our family web site which contains links to Jonathan's original web site and to his university dissertation. There is also a site dedicated to this book giving some background information on Jonathan and Brenda.

http://www.familykay.net
http://www.staringatceilings.co.uk

Email: staring@familykay.net